# WHAT'S MY SUPERPOWER?

## DISCOVERING YOUR UNIQUE TALENTS

WRITTEN
BY
**DELANDA
COLEMAN
&
TERRENCE
COLEMAN**

ILLUSTRATED
BY
**BOWEN
JIANG**

Sydney & Coleman

Illustrations by Bowen Jiang
Cover and Book Design by Leslie Carol

Hardback ISBN 978-1-7344158-6-5
Paperback ISBN 978-1-7344158-5-8
eBook ISBN 978-1-7344158-7-2

Library of Congress Control Number: 2020920099

First Edition February, 2021

Published by Sydney and Coleman, LLC
www.sydneyandcoleman.com
Boston, Massachusetts
Instagram and Facebook @sydneyandcoleman

S.S. COLEMAN
S.K COLEMAN
Victor Prime Sr.
SuperPower Formulas FOR MORTALS
L.D. COLEMAN
K.Nixon
W. Sydney

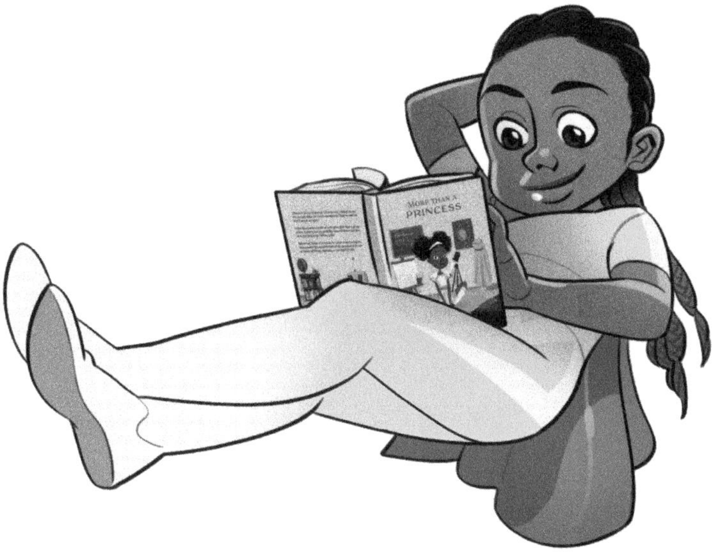
MORE THAN A
PRINCESS

# THIS BOOK IS DEDICATED

TO OUR VERY OWN SUPERHERO, SYDNEY.

YOU ARE SMART, BRAVE AND UNSTOPPABLE.

WE KNOW YOU ARE GOING TO CHANGE THE WORLD.

LOVE ALWAYS,
MOM & DAD

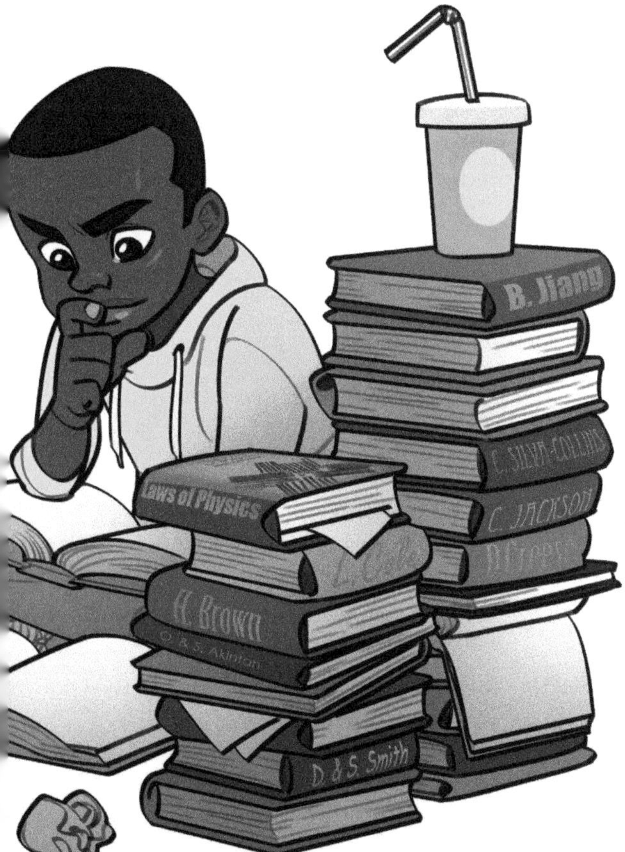
B. Jiang
C. SILVA-COLLINS
Laws of Physics
C. JACKSON
H. Brown
D. & S. Smith

# JOIN OUR DIGITAL BOOK CLUB!

After you read this book, we'd like to give you a place to start more adventures with the characters in the Sydney and Coleman collection!

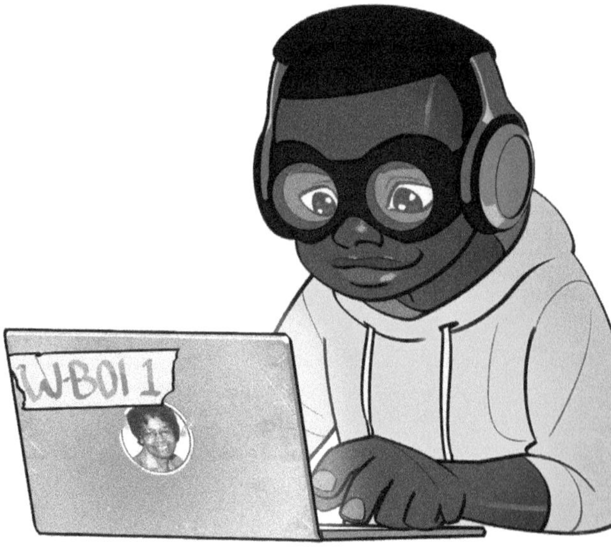
WB01 1

**WE HAVE CREATED A FREE DIGITAL BOOK CLUB THAT YOU CAN ACCESS WHEN YOU VISIT: CLUB.SYDNEYANDCOLEMAN.COM**

## INSIDE THE CLUB, YOU'LL FIND:

- **FREE** activity and coloring pages
- **PREVIEW** of future books and products
- **MEMBERS** only offers!
- **EXCLUSIVE** author readings of all our books
- **DISCOUNT** codes for products offered at SydneyandColeman.com

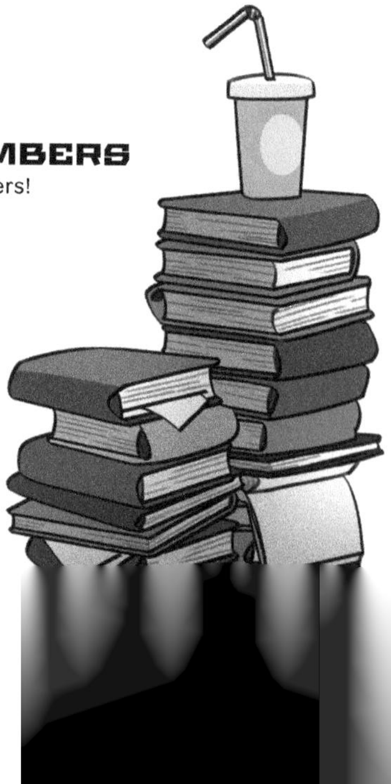

YOU GOT THIS!
GO AWAY, I'M READING
I'm a robot

WHAT'S MY SUPERPOWER?

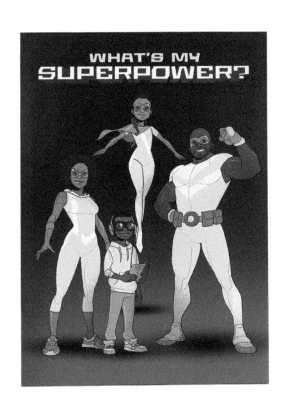

JOIN THE DIGITAL BOOK CLUB FOR YOUR SPECIAL CONTENT!

MORE THAN A PRINCESS
By Delando Coleman & Terrence Coleman

WHAT'S MY SUPERPOWER?

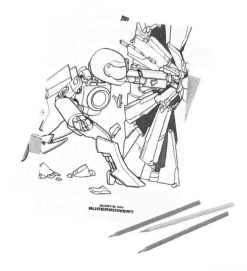

CLUB.SYDNEYANDCOLEMAN.COM

**DESHAUN PRIME** didn't know what to do,

"MY FAMILY IS SPECIAL, HOW I WISH I COULD BE TOO!"

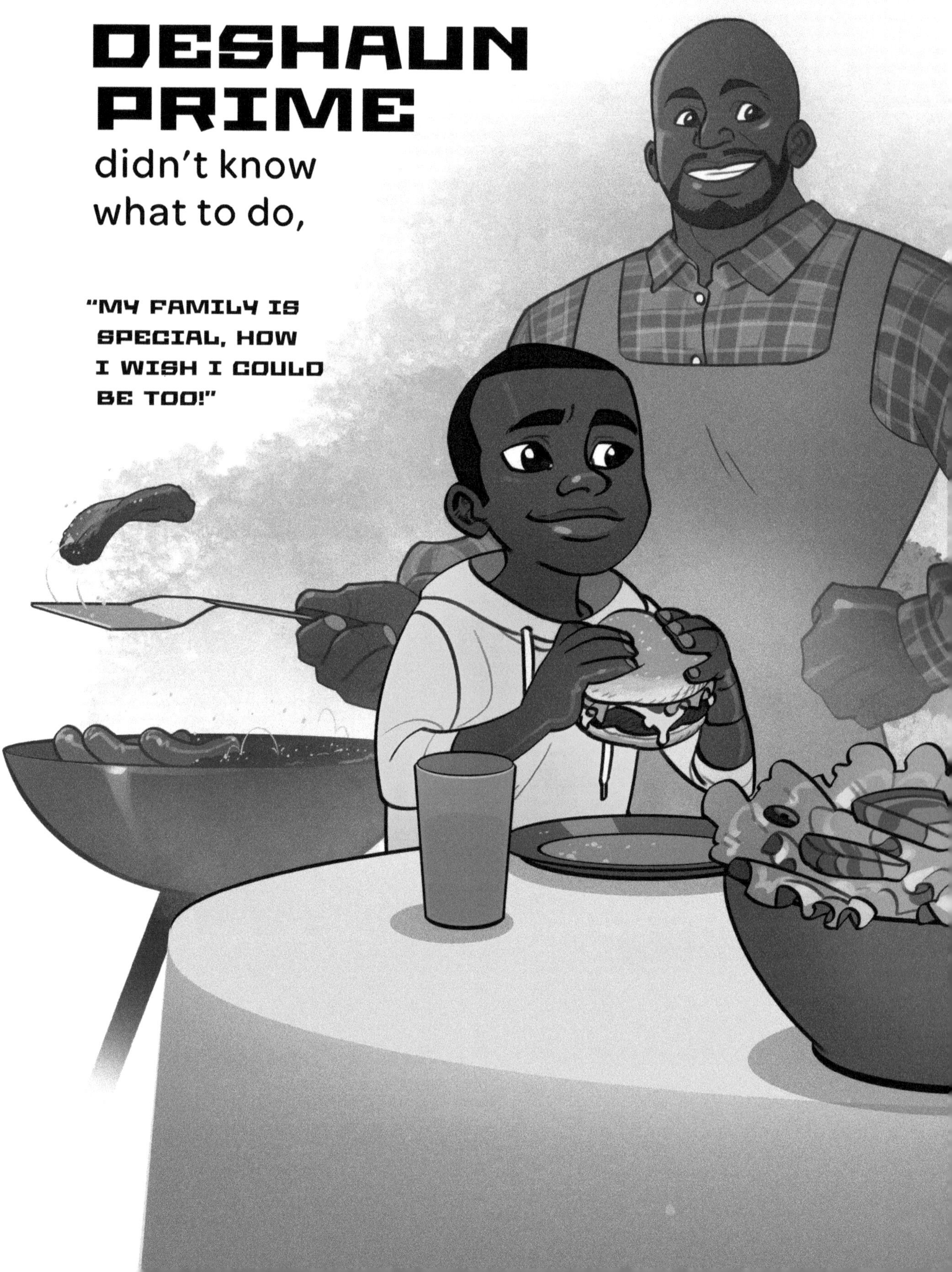

To everyone, his **FAMILY** seemed rather ordinary.

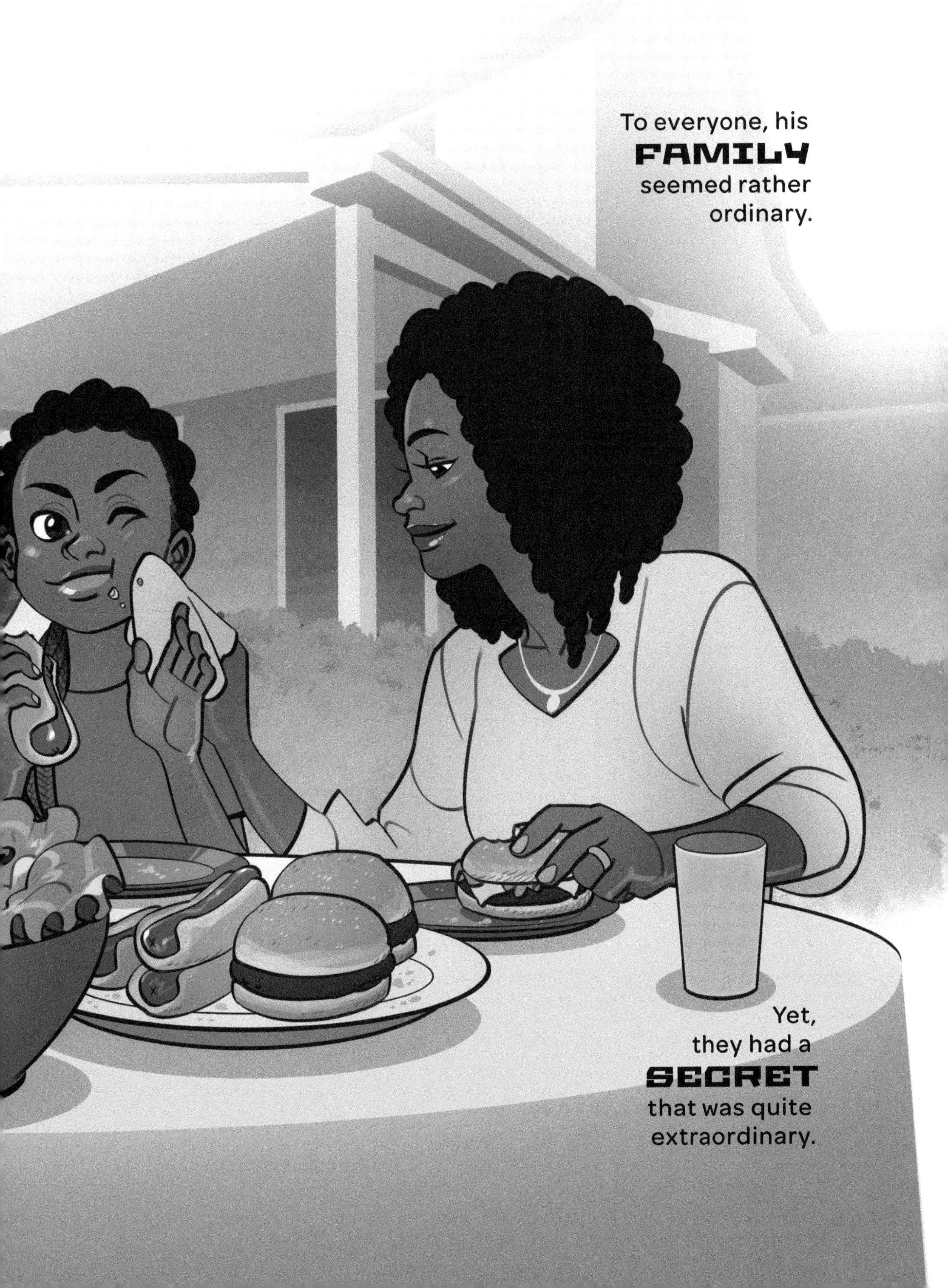

Yet, they had a **SECRET** that was quite extraordinary.

Deshaun lived with his Mom and Dad, and little sister **JANET.**

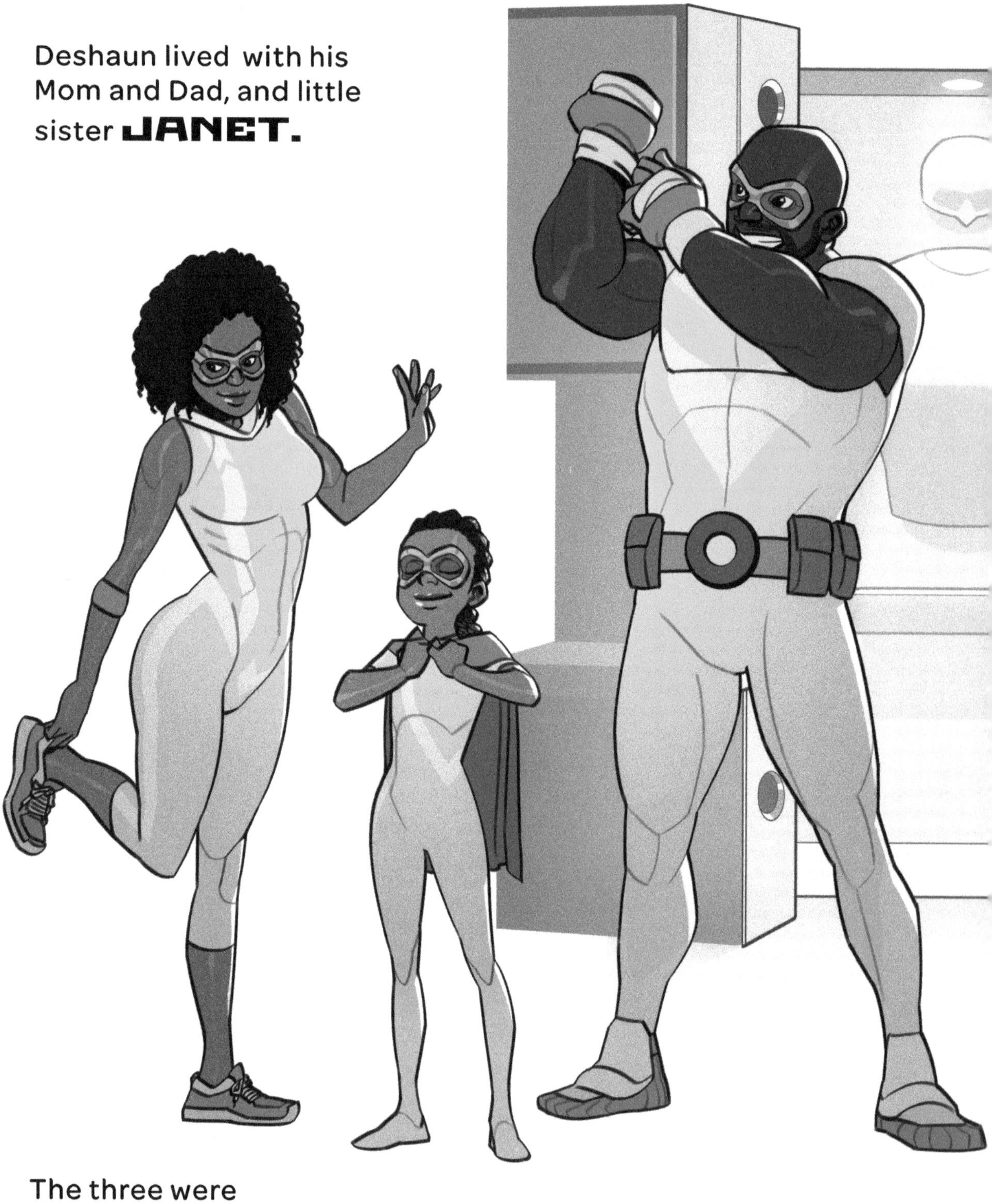

The three were

**SUPERHEROES**

and they often saved the planet.

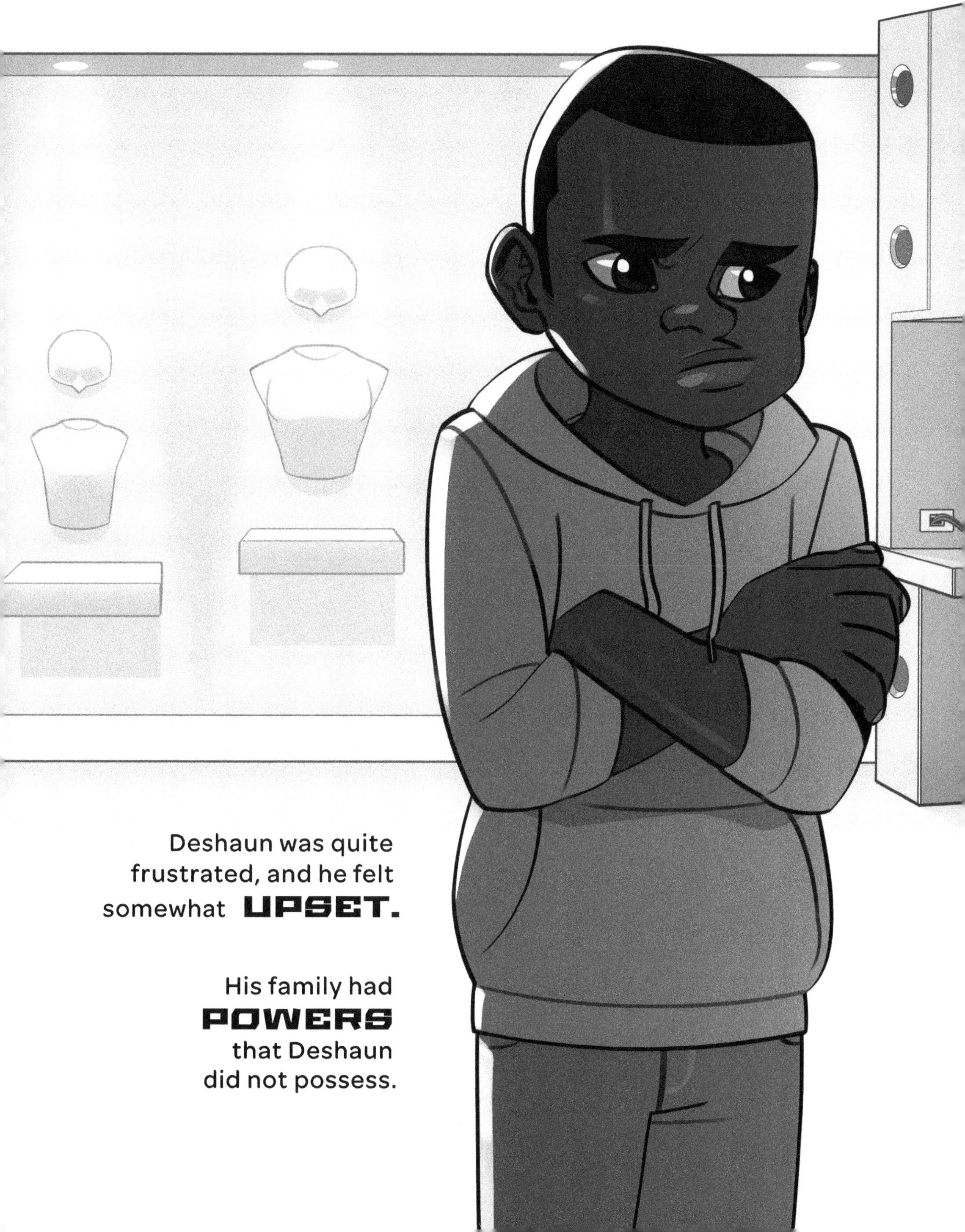

Deshaun was quite frustrated, and he felt somewhat **UPSET.**

His family had **POWERS** that Deshaun did not possess.

His Dad was super
**STRONG,**
his skin as thick as
heavy lead.

He punched down
big, thick walls
and lifted cars
above his
head.

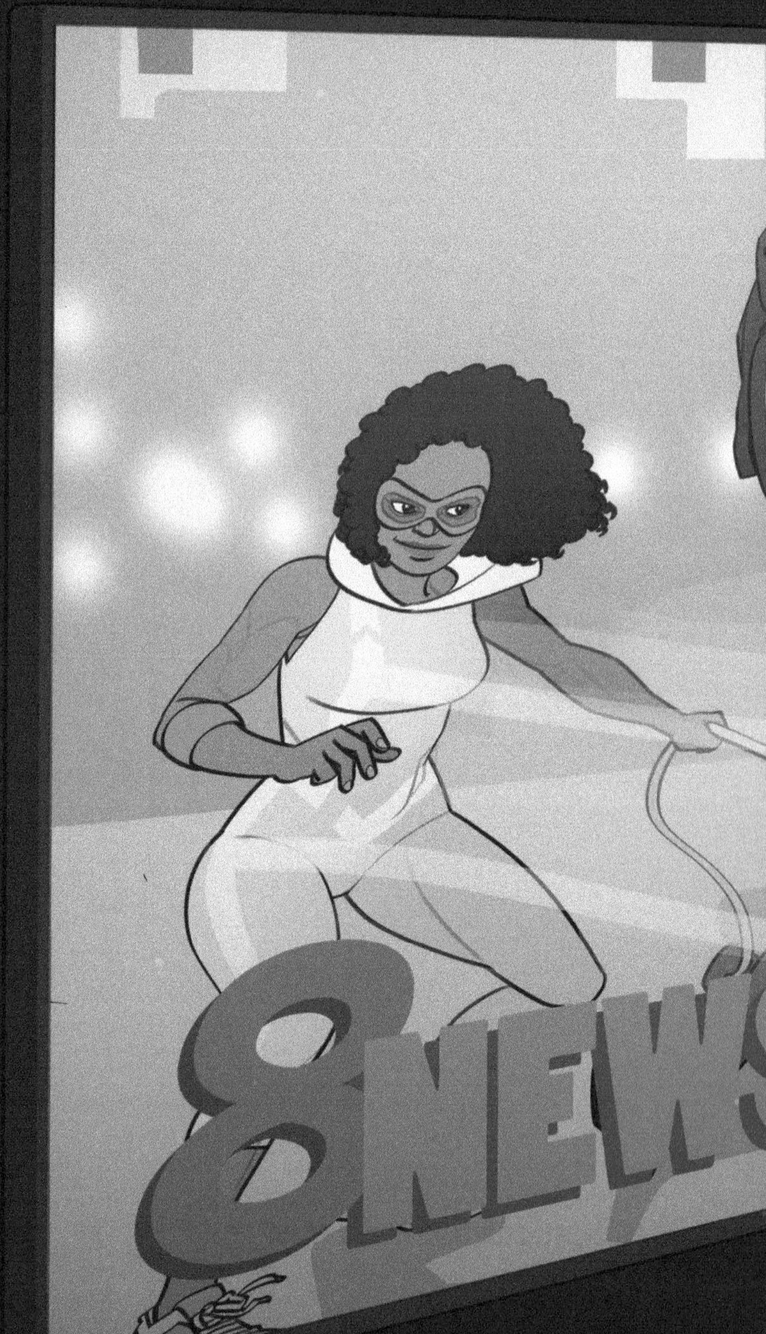
8NEWS

His Mom
could run
from east to
west in less than
half a minute.

She was the
**FASTEST** in the world,
her runs had no speed limit!

He tried to jump up high
so he could also
fly around,

But one wrong
step and

**"OUCH!"**

he took a tumble
to the ground!

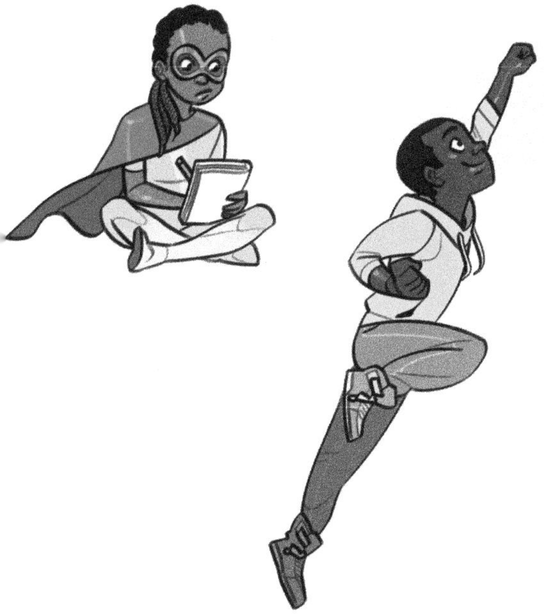

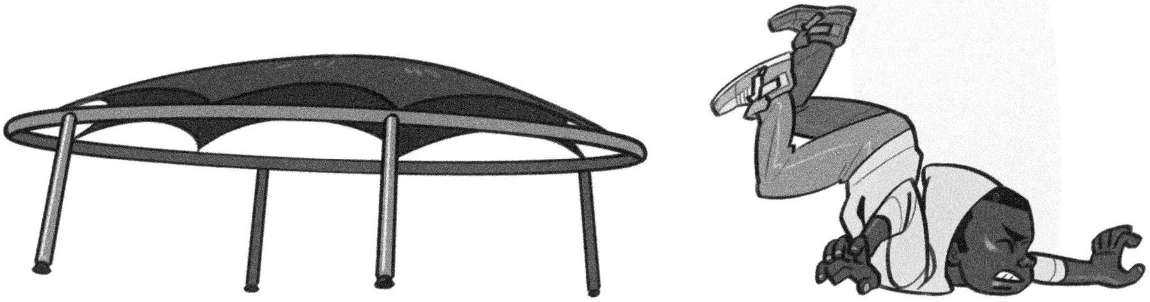

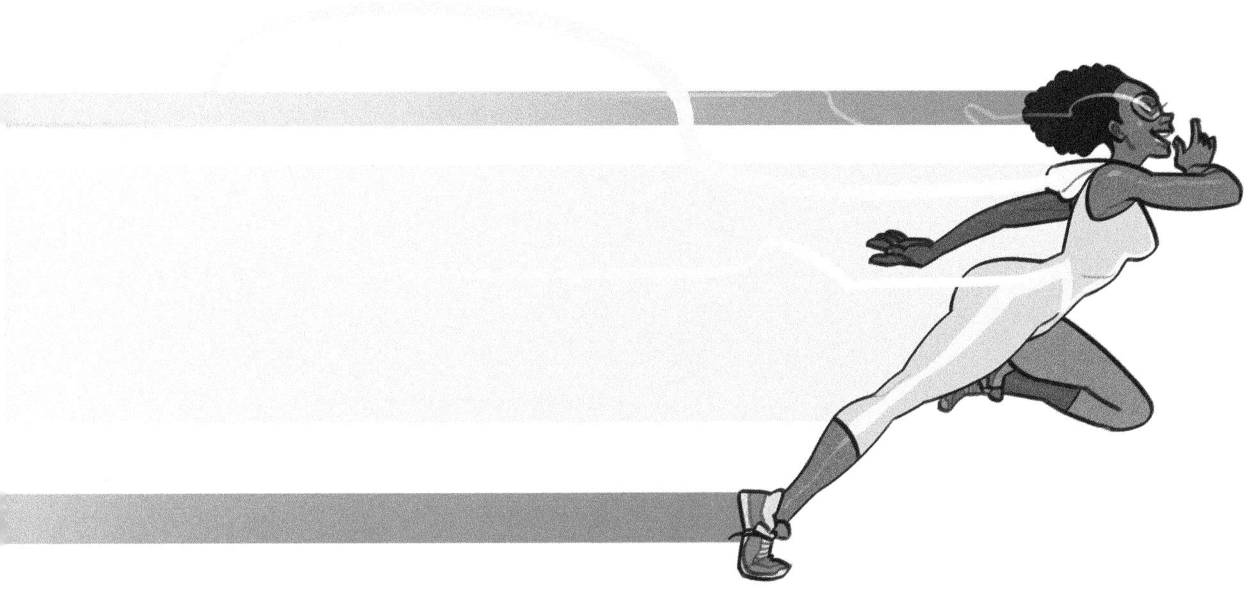

His parents pulled
Deshaun aside,
they noticed his
**SAD MOOD.**

They were a bit
**CONCERNED**
about his dismal attitude.

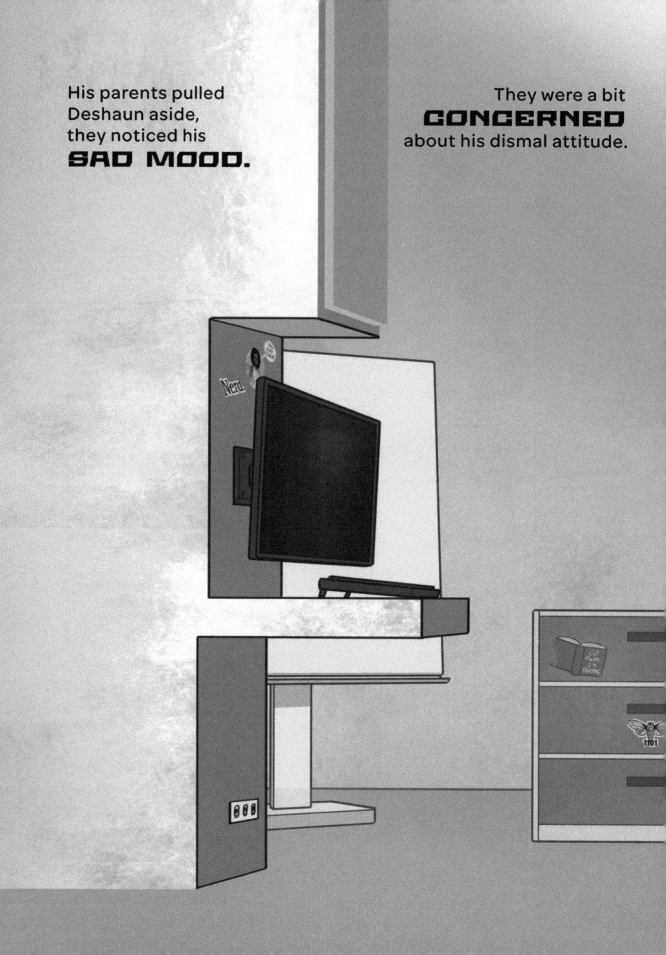

His Mom and Dad said,
"Sweetheart, try to be
more optimistic,"
everyone has
superpowers.
All of us are
**GIFTED."**

"The world one day will need
a deed that only you can do.

So, **FOCUS** on
the things that feel
more natural
to you."

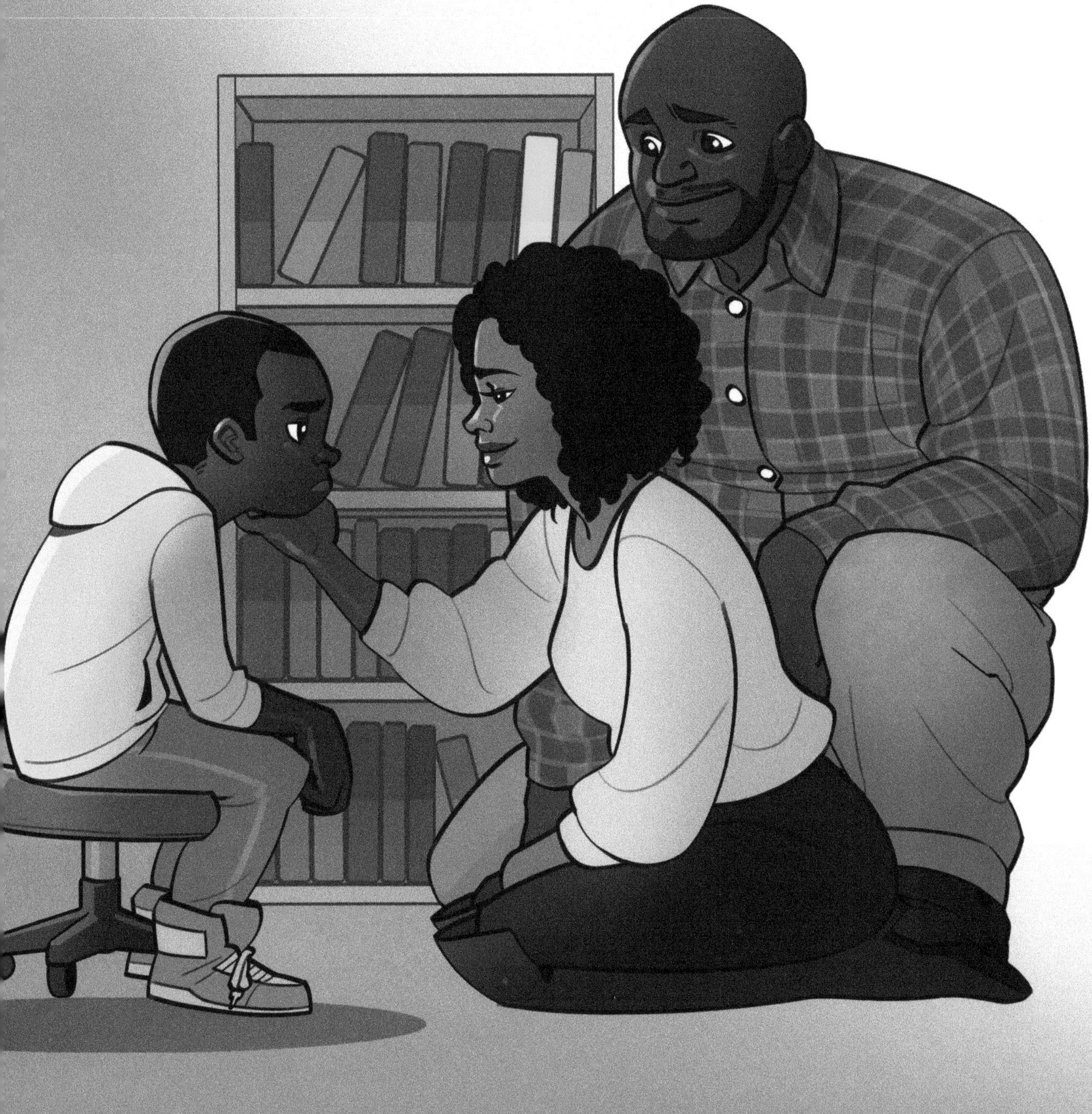

Deshaun began to wonder what his **GIFT** could really be.

He wanted to be like his parents and help all those in need.

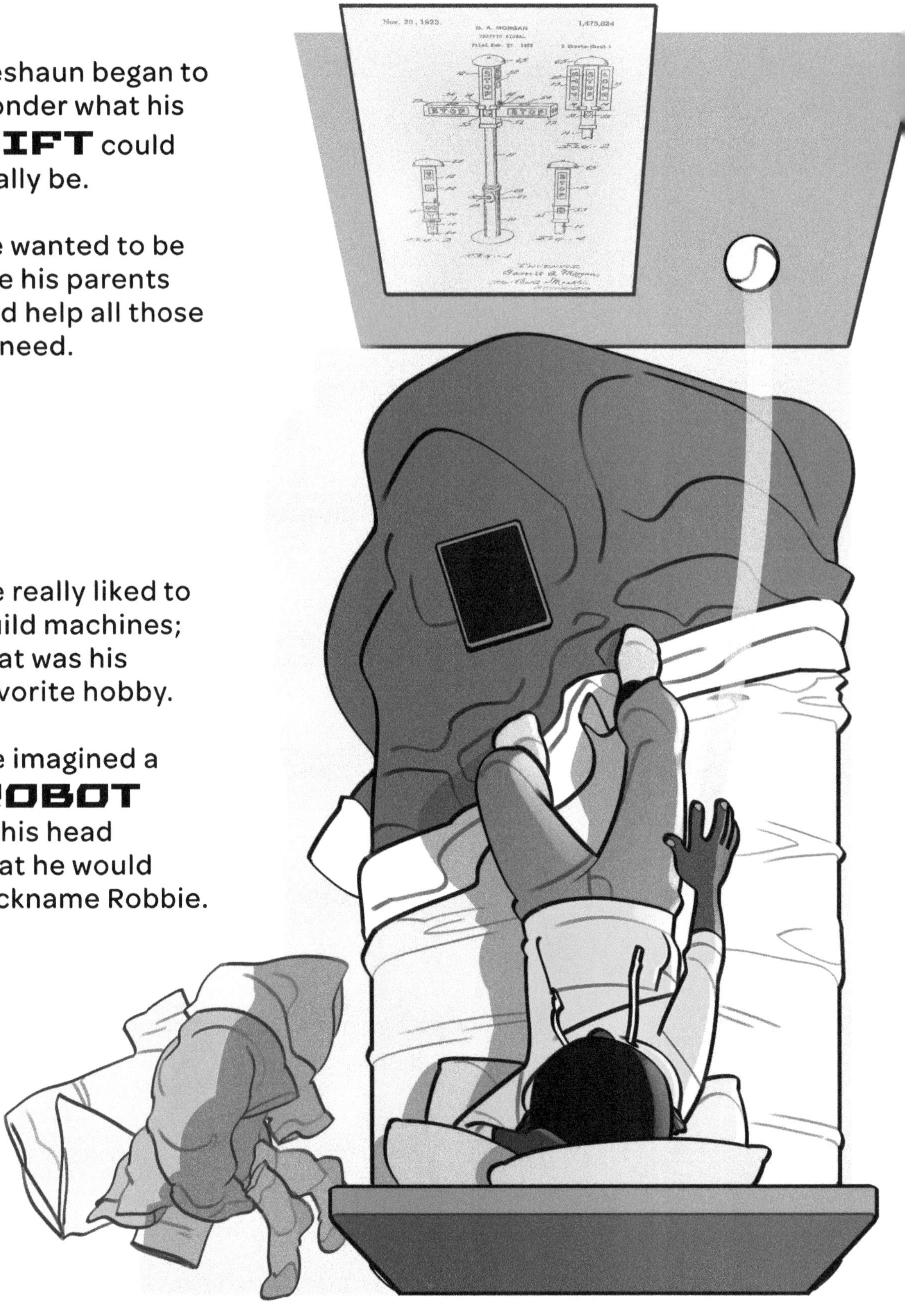

Nov. 20, 1923.
G. A. MORGAN
1,475,024
STOP


He really liked to build machines; that was his favorite hobby.

He imagined a **ROBOT** in his head that he would nickname Robbie.

**"ROBBIE WILL COMBINE THE GIFTS OF MOM, DAD AND SIS."**

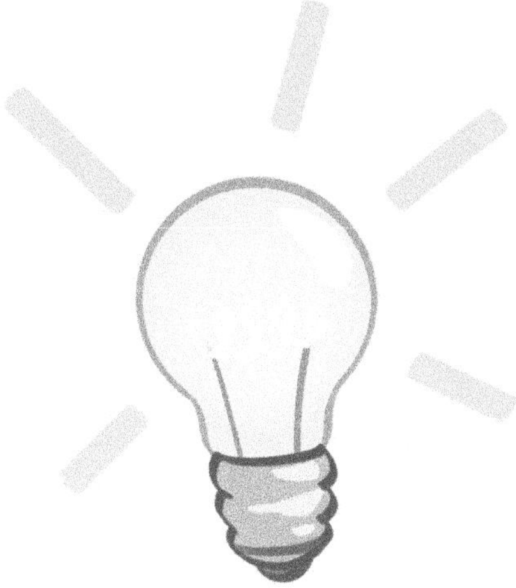

Deshaun became excited just by **THINKING** about this!

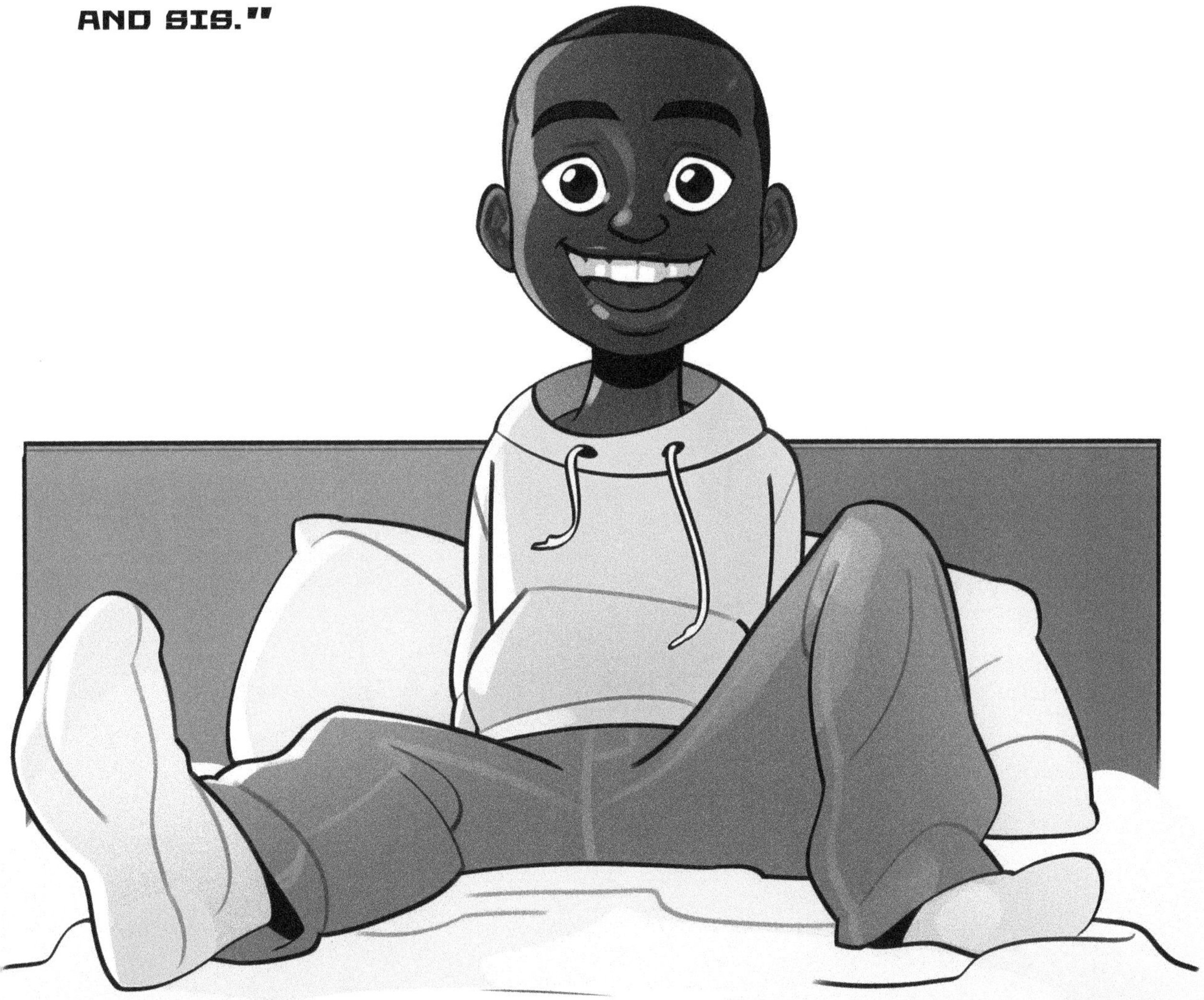

You see, Deshaun was bright
and numerically inclined.
He'd quickly solve
equations just by
focusing his
**MIND.**

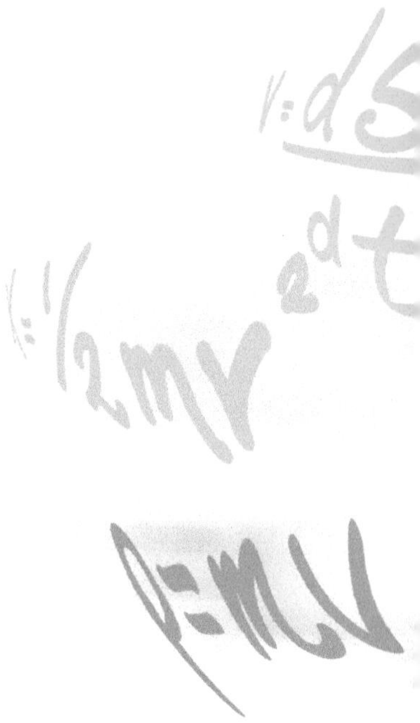

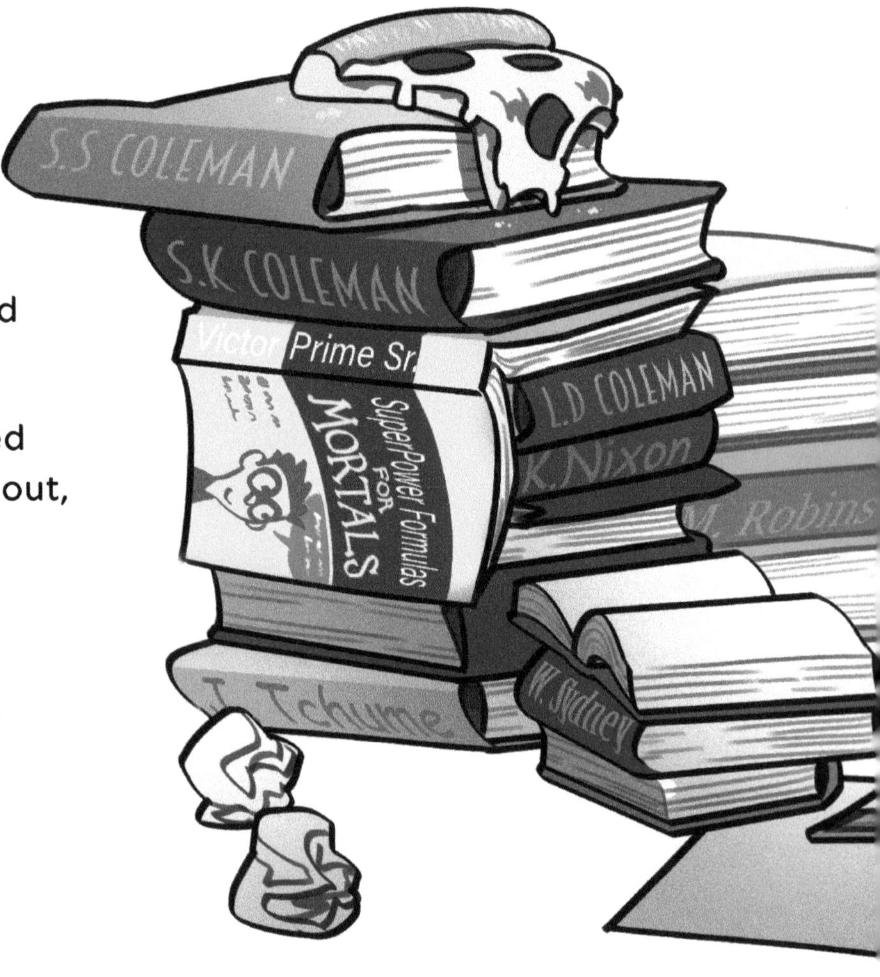
S.S COLEMAN
S.K COLEMAN
Victor Prime Sr.
SuperPower Formulas FOR MORTALS
L.D COLEMAN
K.Nixon
M. Robins
J. Tchume
W. Sydney

While others
would take days,
Deshaun could read
a book in hours.

And he remembered
all he **READ** about,
like speed, flight,
and power.

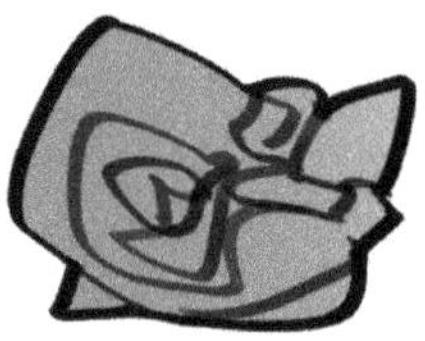

He **LEARNED** about these concepts in a book called: Laws of Physics.

Power, speed, and flight are things a machine could mimic.

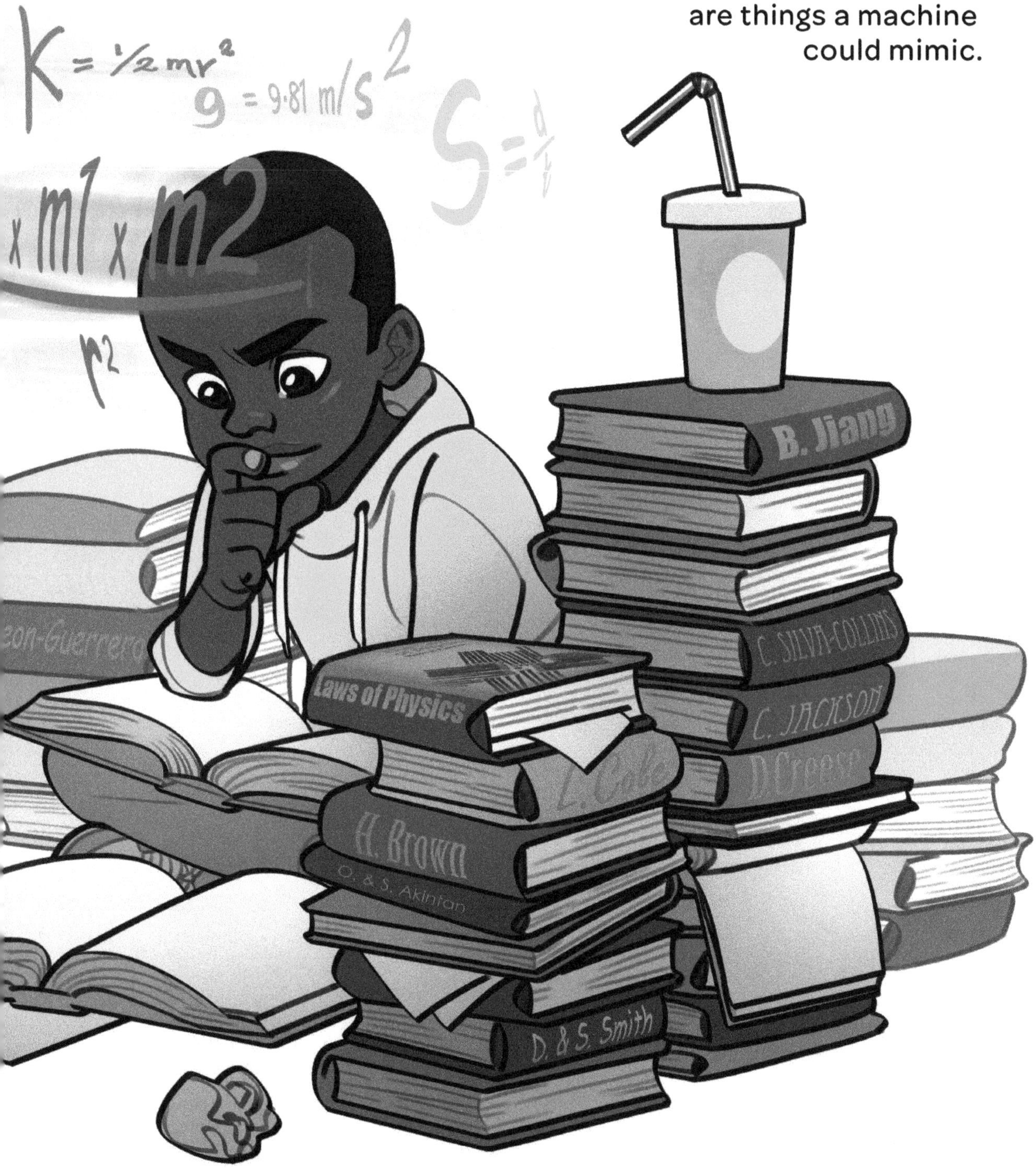
$K = \frac{1}{2}mr^2$
$g = 9.81\ m/s^2$
B. Jiang
C. SILVA-COLLINS
C. JACKSON
Laws of Physics
L. Cole
H. Brown
O. & S. Akinfan
D. & S. Smith

He grabbed his handy
pencil to **SKETCH**
all that it would take.

And soon, he realized
Robbie was something
he could **MAKE!**

**"PIECE OF CAKE!"**

exclaimed Deshaun,

**"NOW, ALL I NEED ARE TOOLS, AND ALL THE MATHEMATICS AND IDEAS I LEARNED IN SCHOOL."**

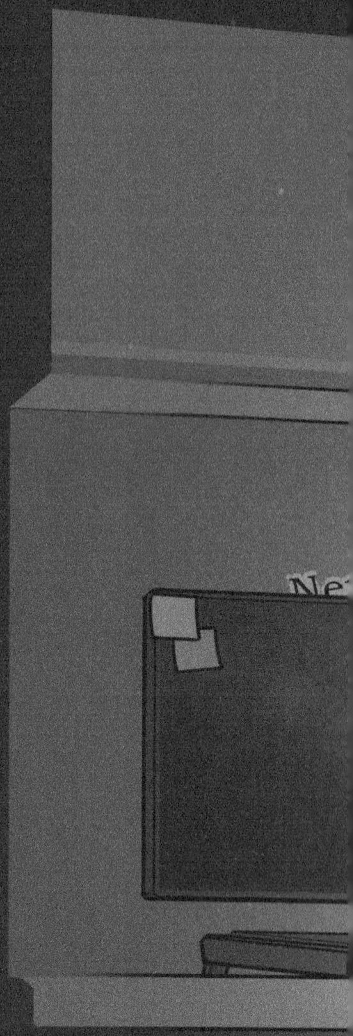

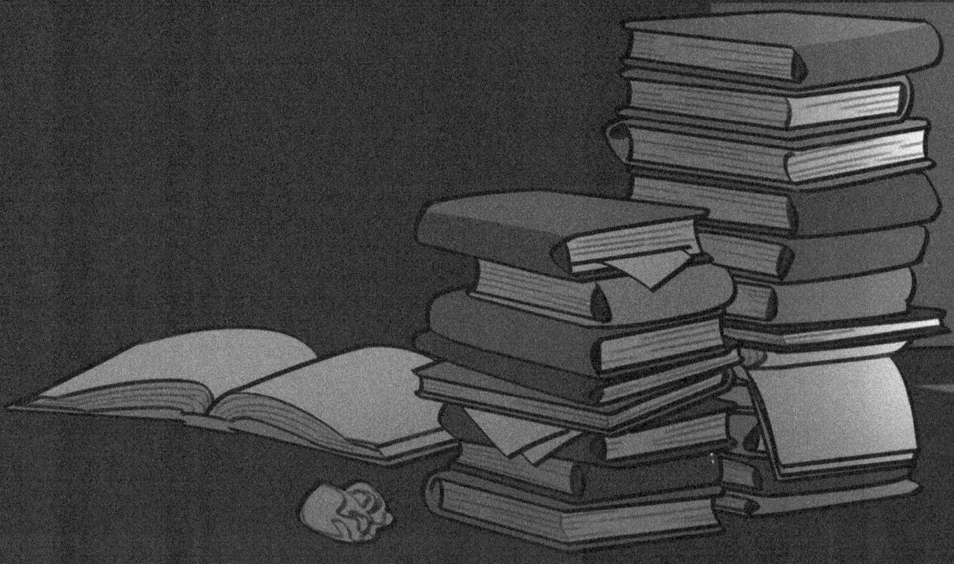

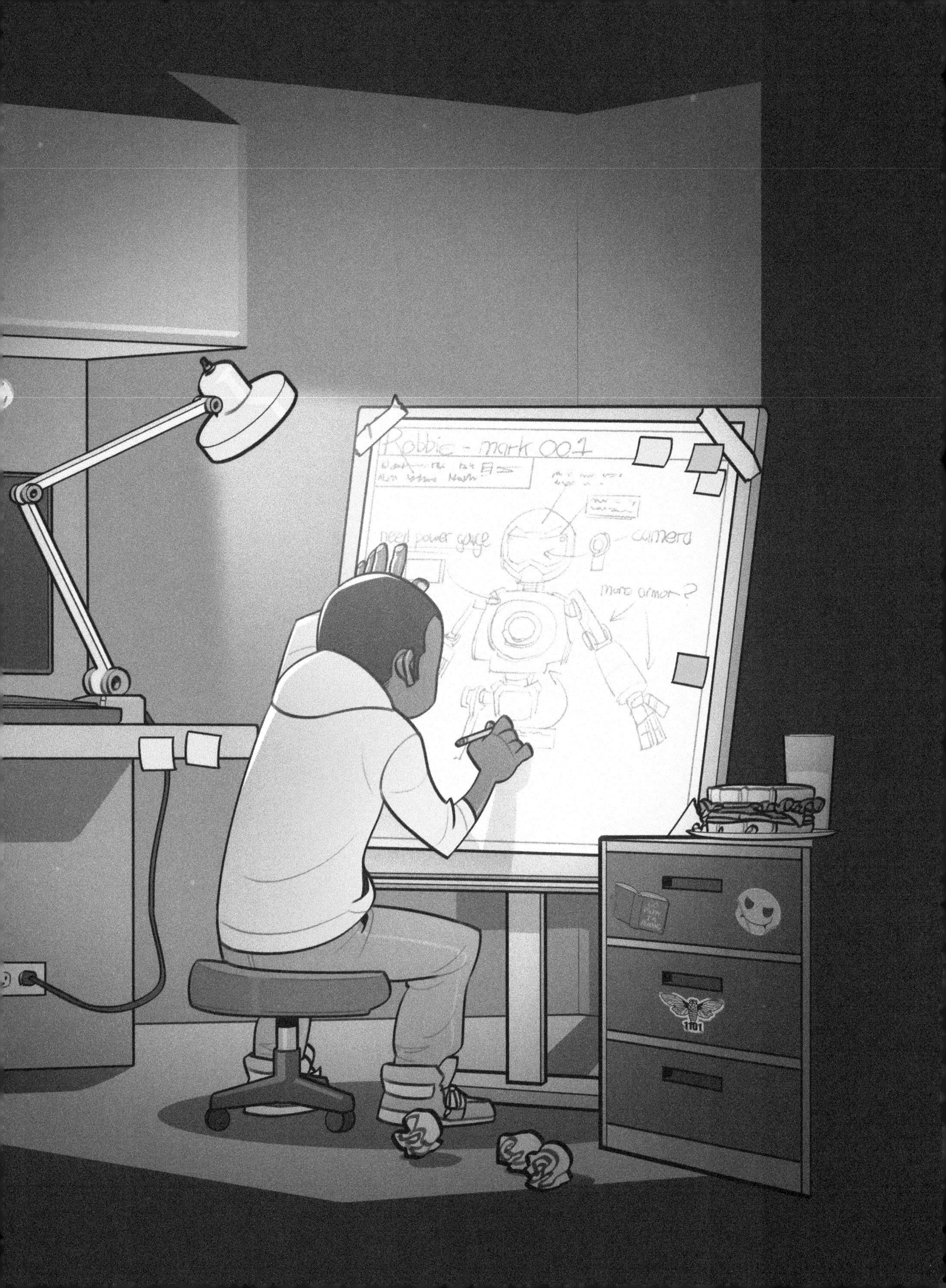

Robbie - mark 001
need power gauge
camera
more armor?

Deshaun began to think
about the things he could
**CONSTRUCT,**

"MY FIRST STEP'S
GETTING STARTED,
THEN I'LL SIMPLY
TEST MY LUCK!"

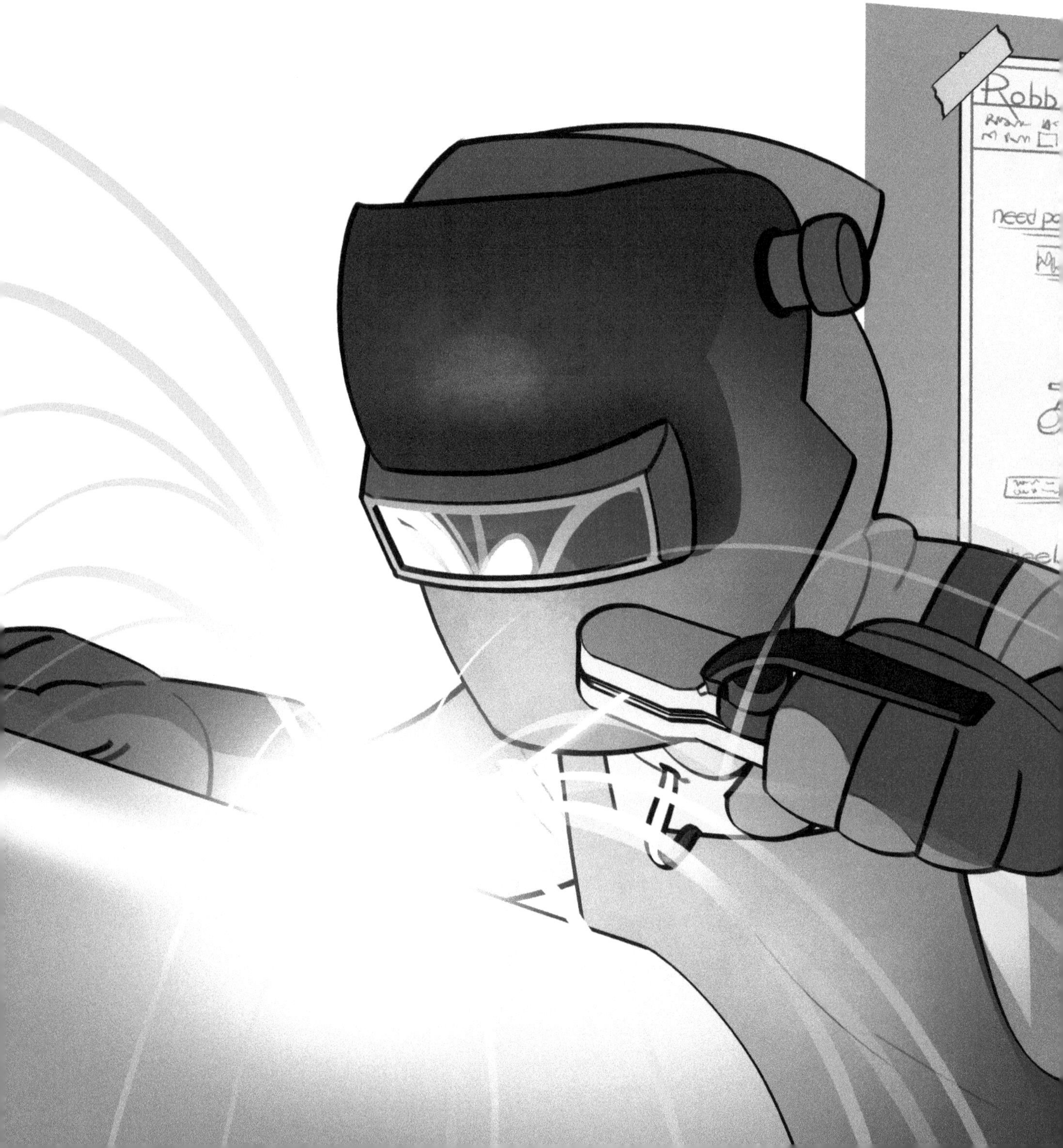

He **TRIED** out different models, day by day and week by week,

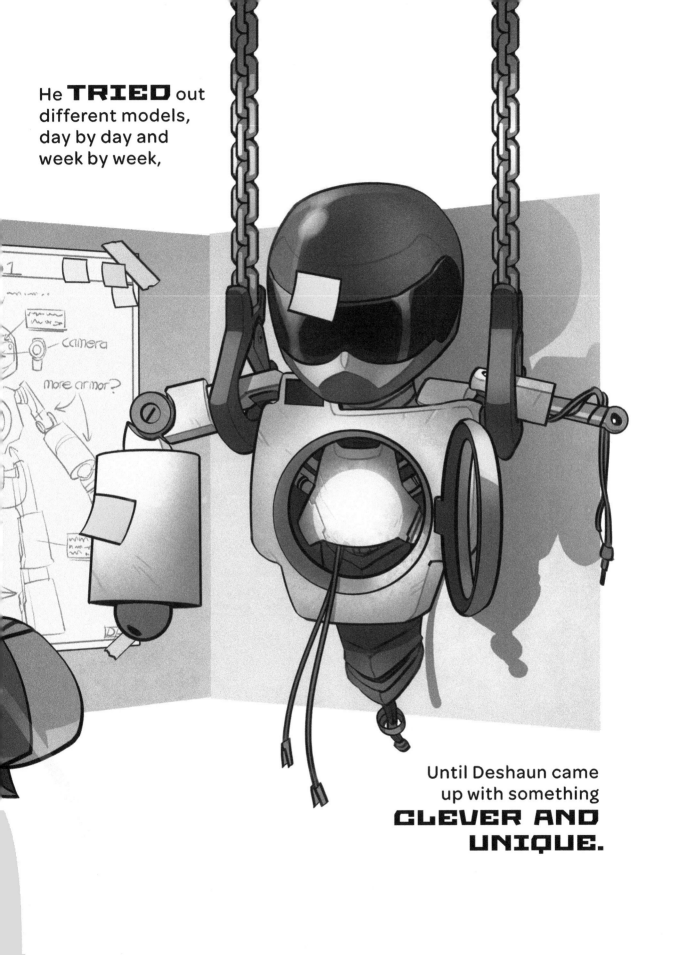

Until Deshaun came up with something **CLEVER AND UNIQUE.**

First, he needed **ROBBIE**
to begin to move around,

He typed in the right
codes, and Robbie
stepped onto
the ground!

Robbie - mark 001
need power gauge
camera
more or not?
wheels?

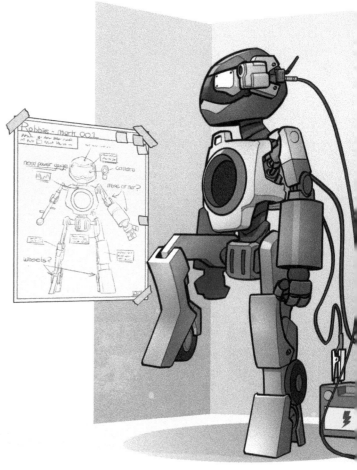

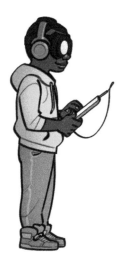

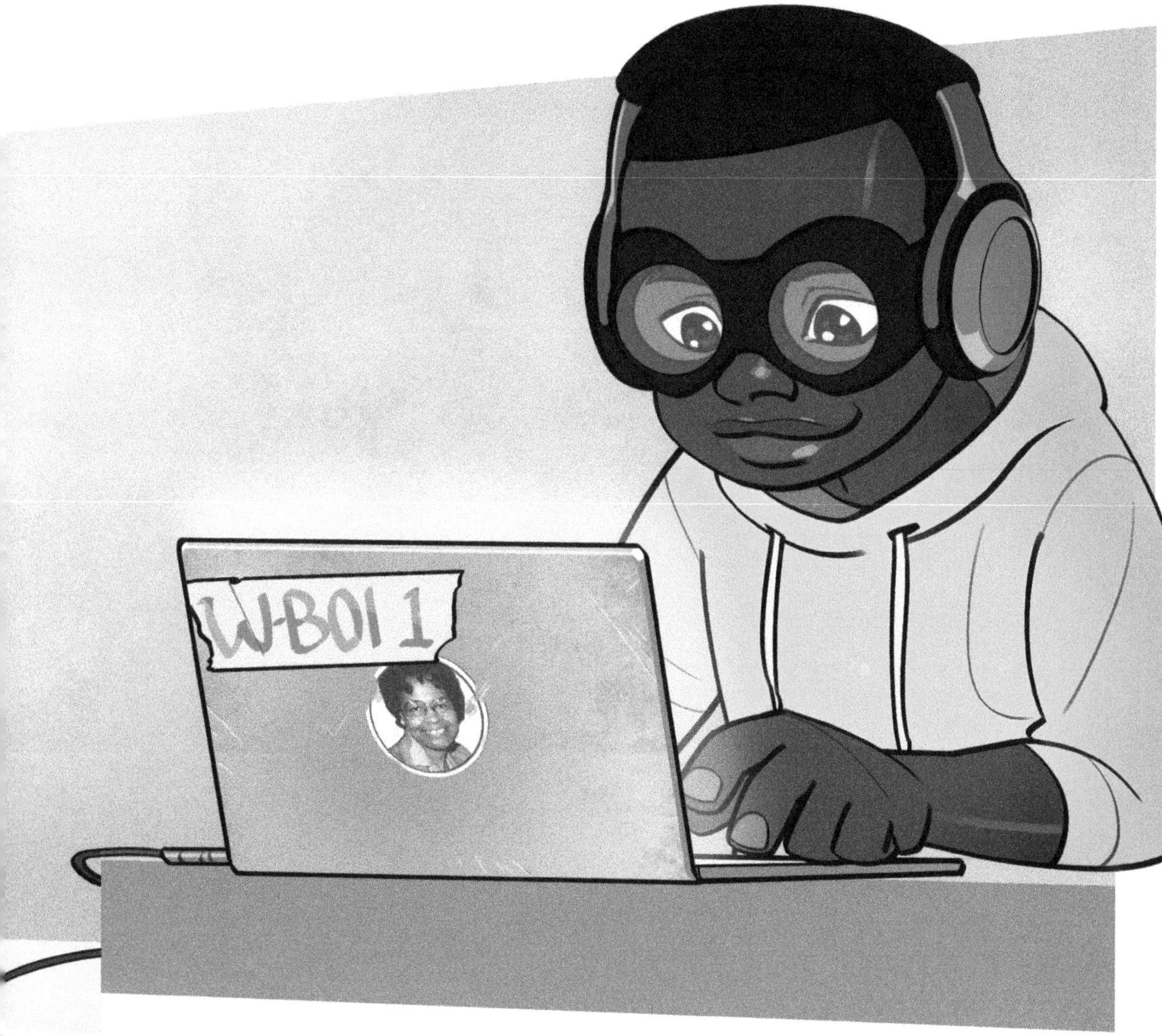

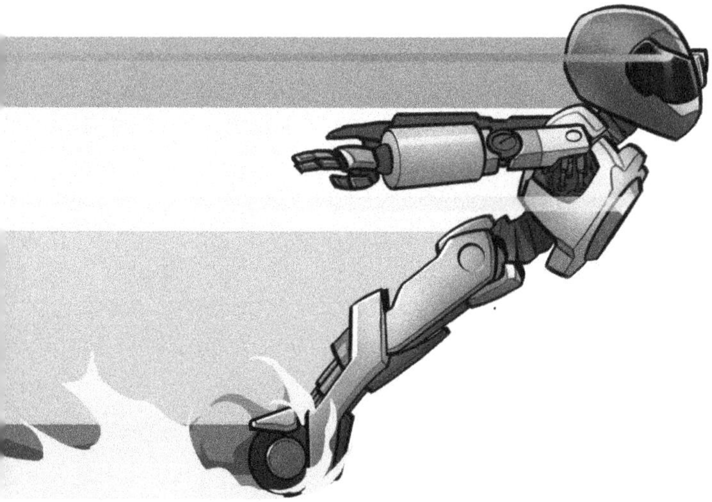

Distance
divided by
time is the
formula for
**SPEED.**

He wanted Robbie to
be fast. Very fast indeed!

Deshaun attached some **ROCKETS,**

**"THEY WILL HELP THE ROBOT TRAVEL."**

But rockets cause pollution and the atmosphere is fragile.

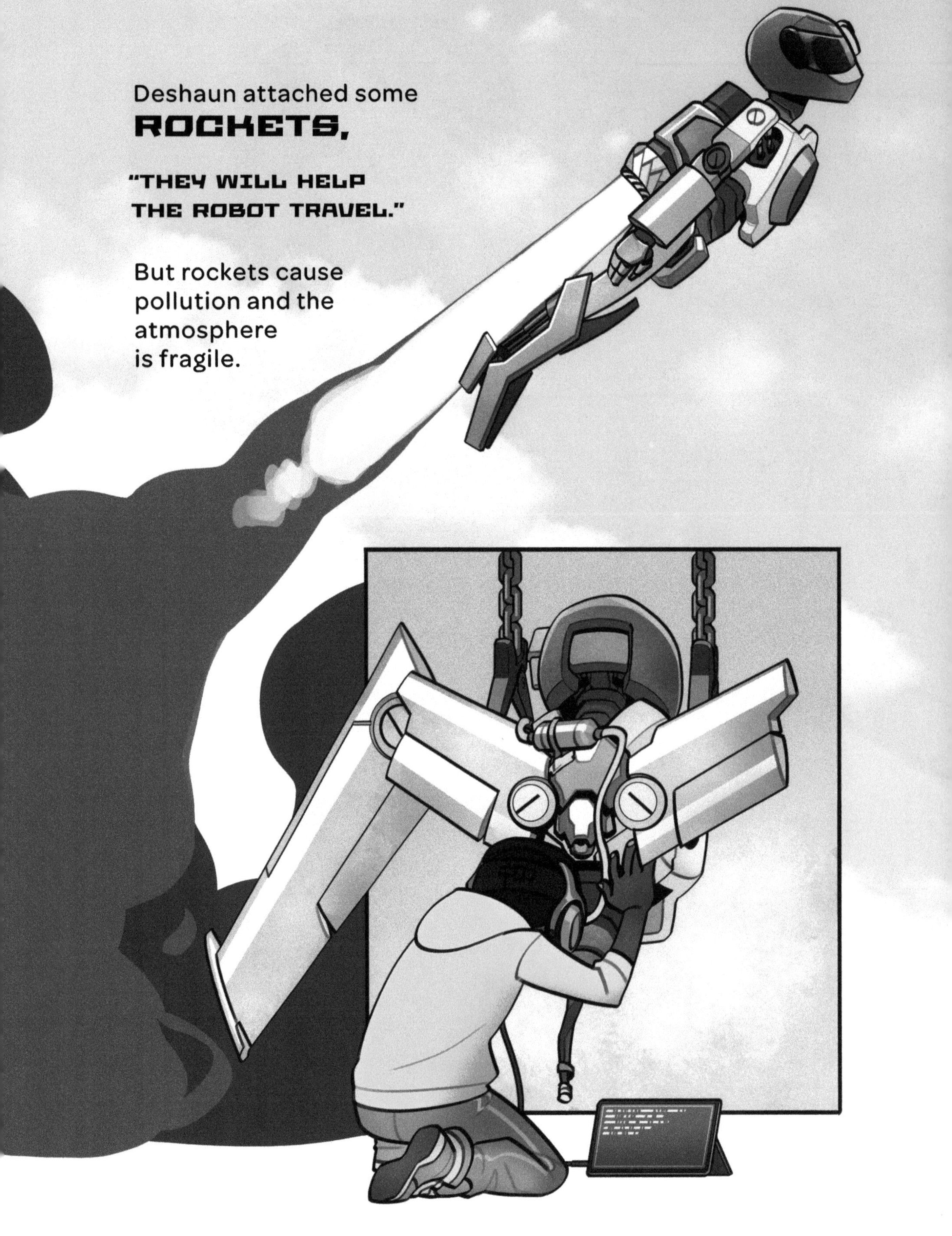

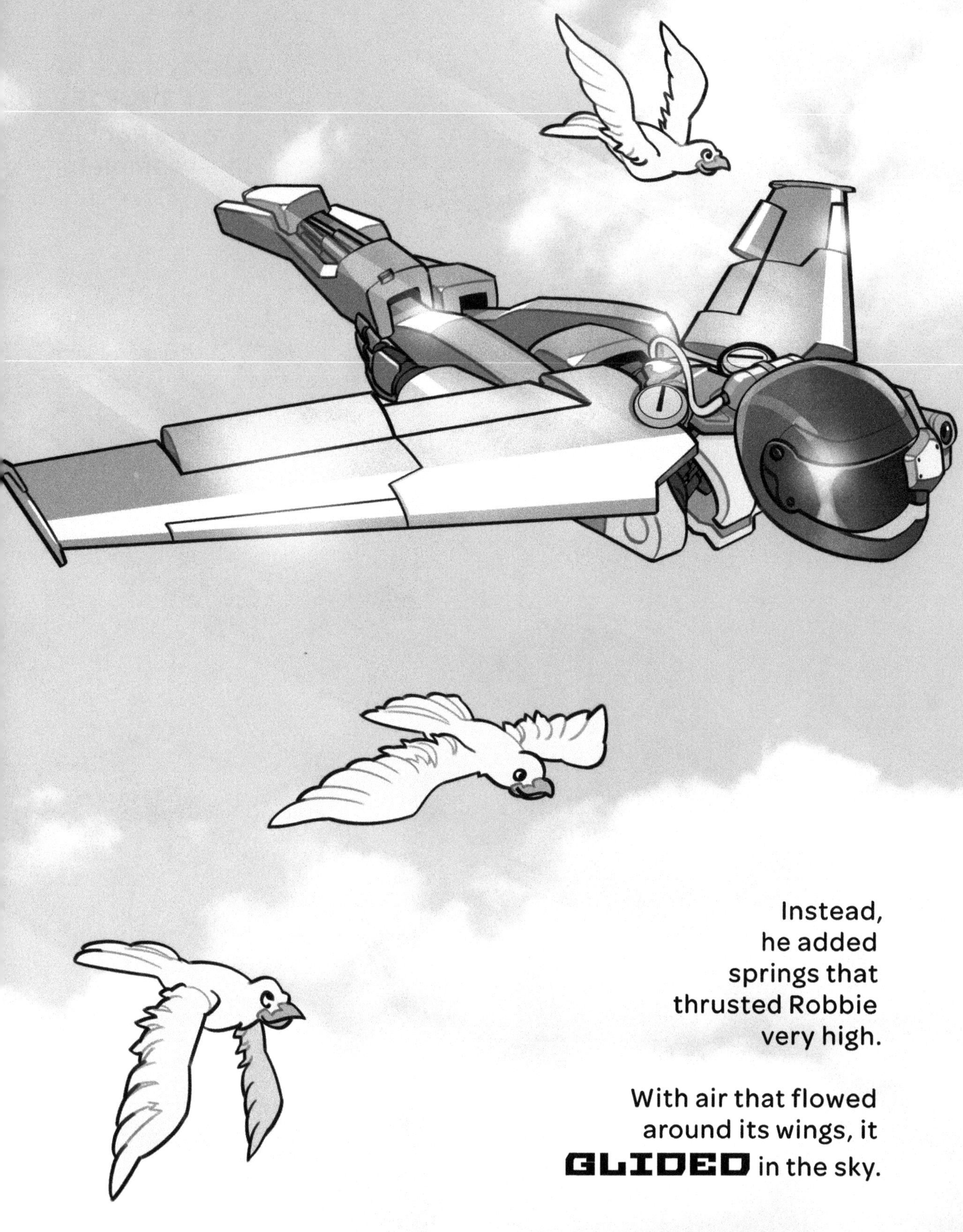

Instead,
he added
springs that
thrusted Robbie
very high.

With air that flowed
around its wings, it
**GLIDED** in the sky.

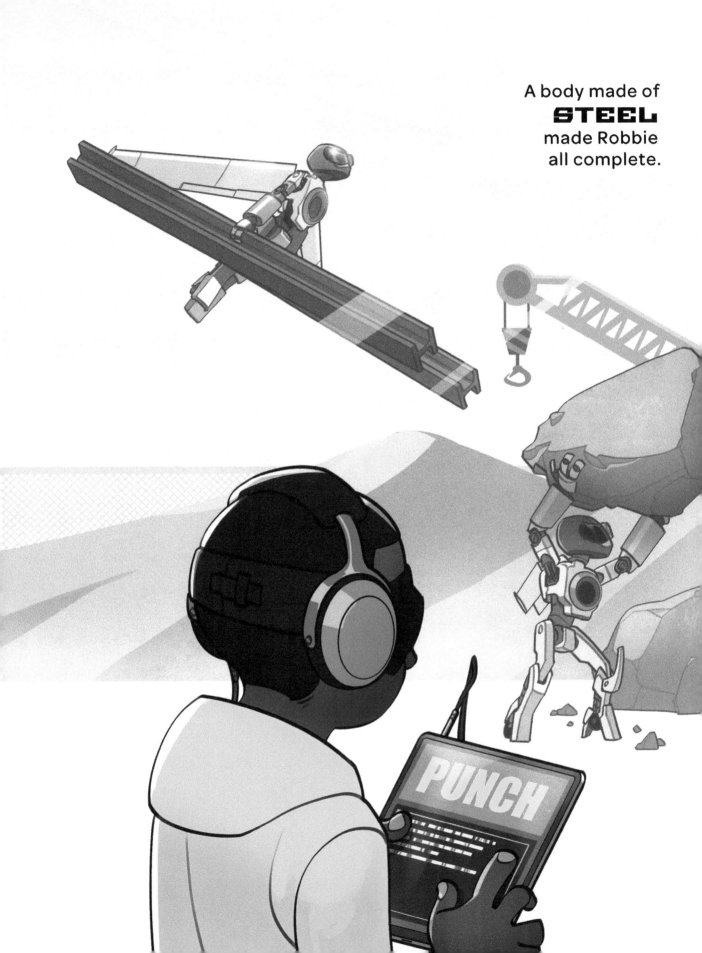

A body made of
**STEEL**
made Robbie
all complete.

The arms could lift up boulders and **PUNCH** holes through concrete.

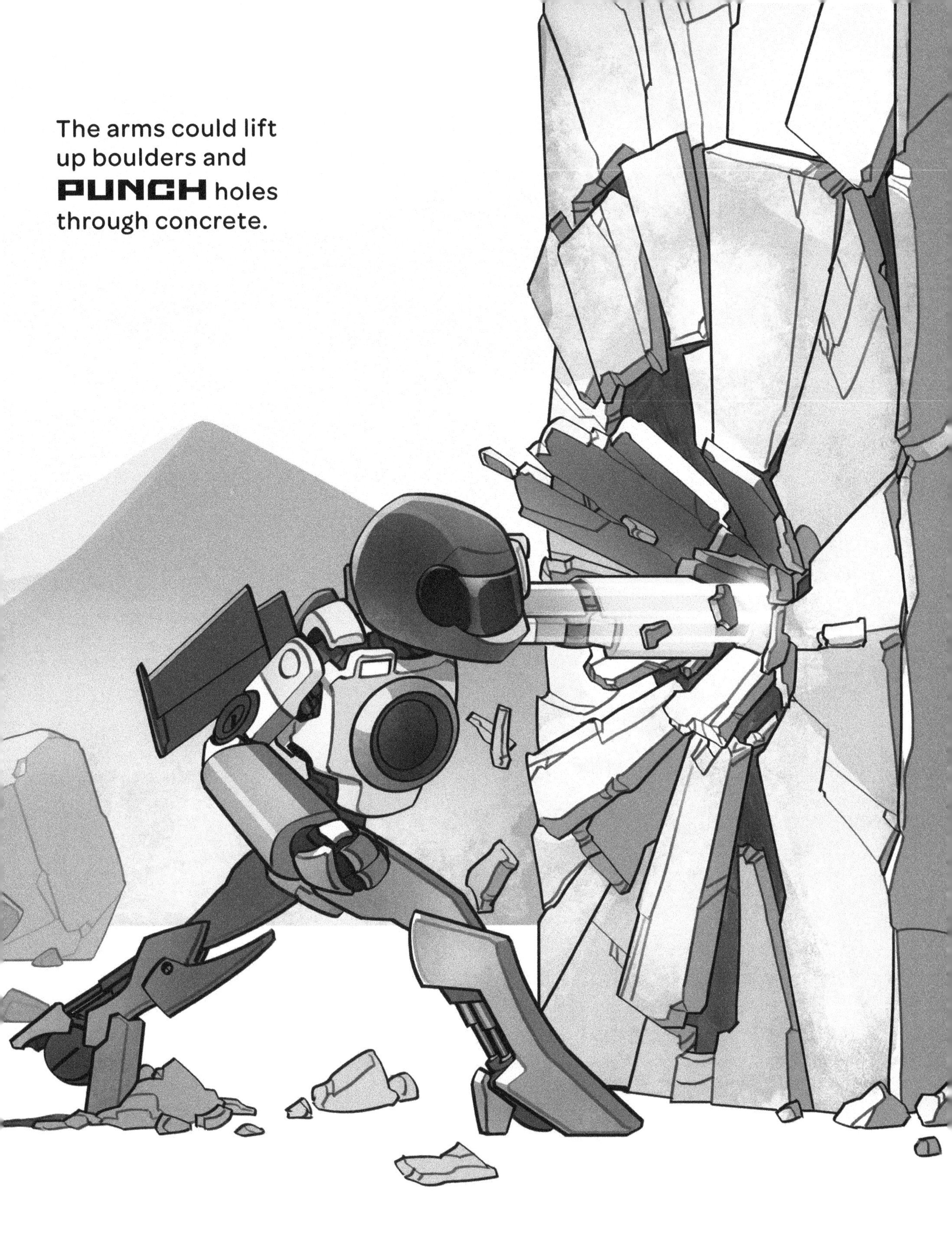

His parents came to check on him and said, "We're so **IMPRESSED!"**

Even Janet **PRAISED** Deshaun, who proudly swelled his chest.

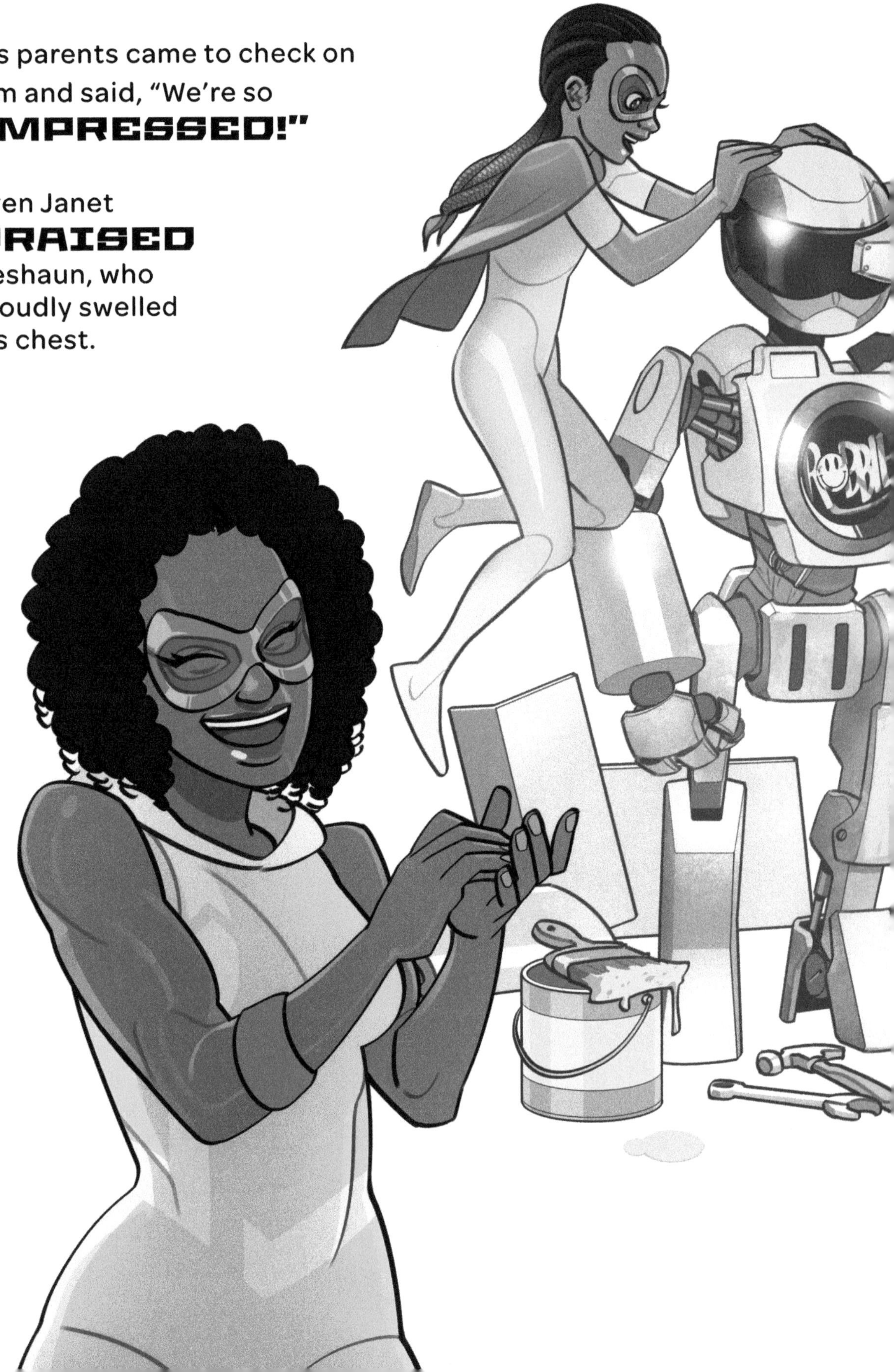

The robot was
**COMPLETED**
and creatively
designed.

"I knew it all along,"
said Dad, "Your
power is your
**MIND!"**

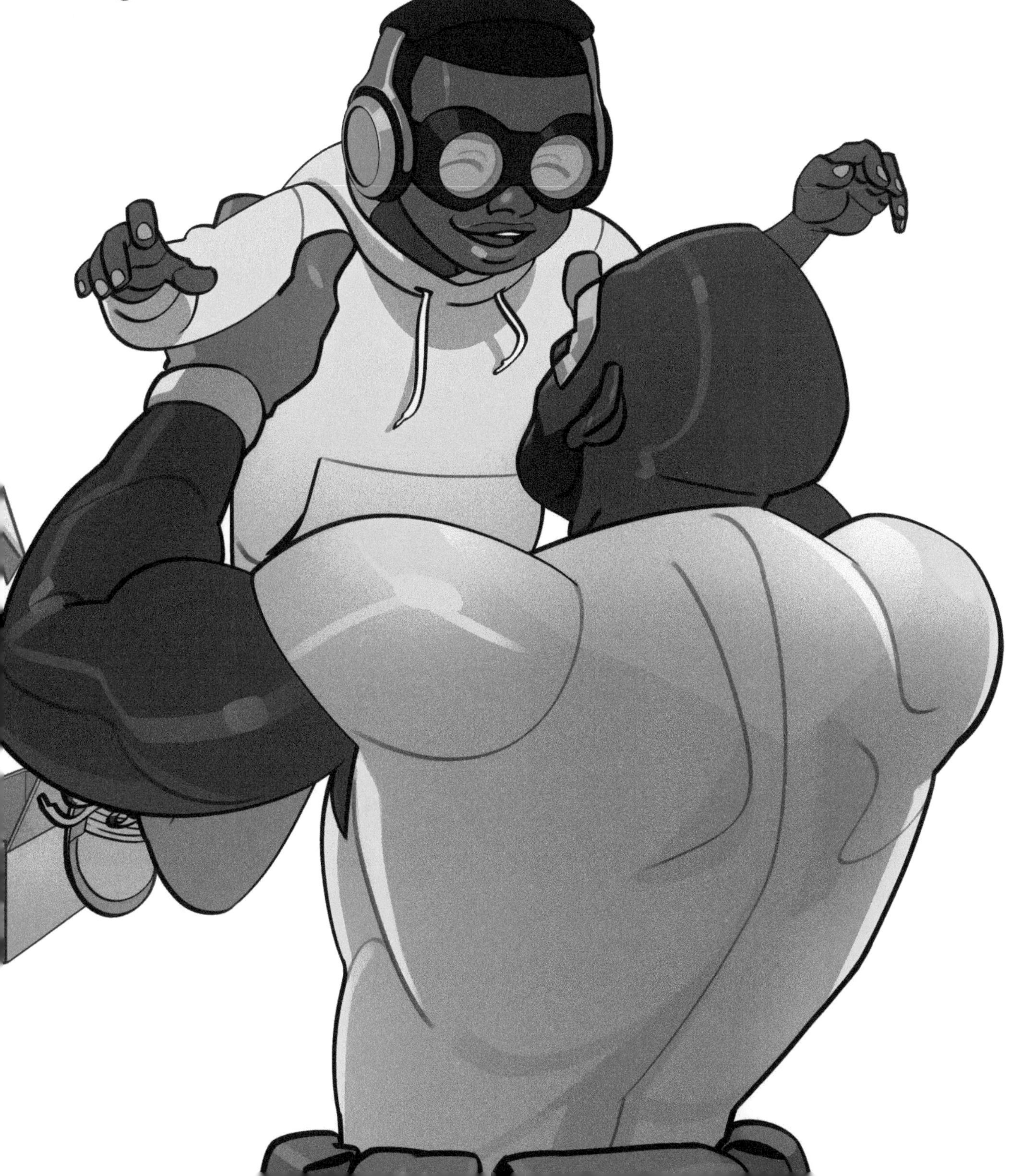

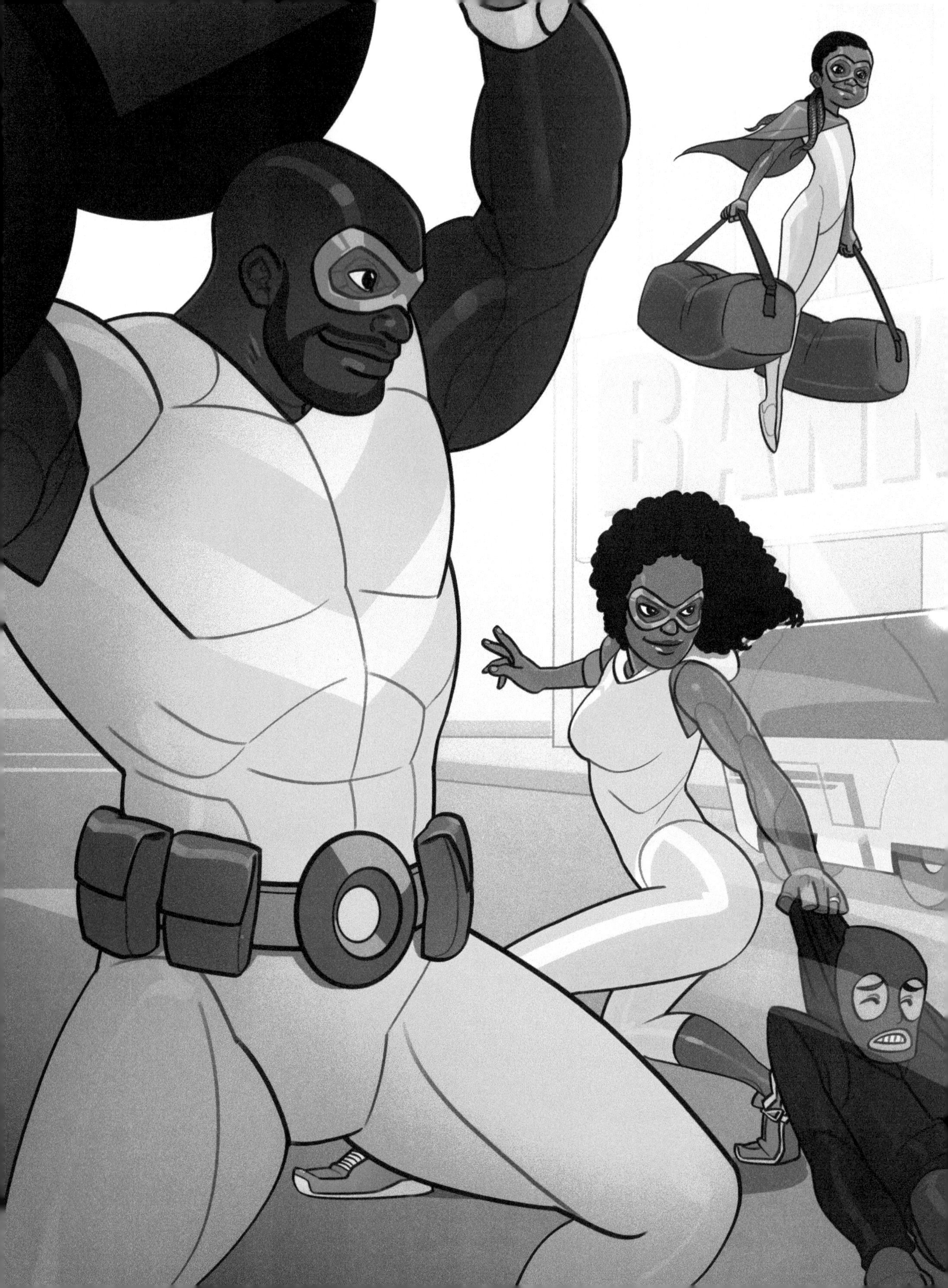

Deshaun was overjoyed.
Now his inventions
**HELPED**
the team!

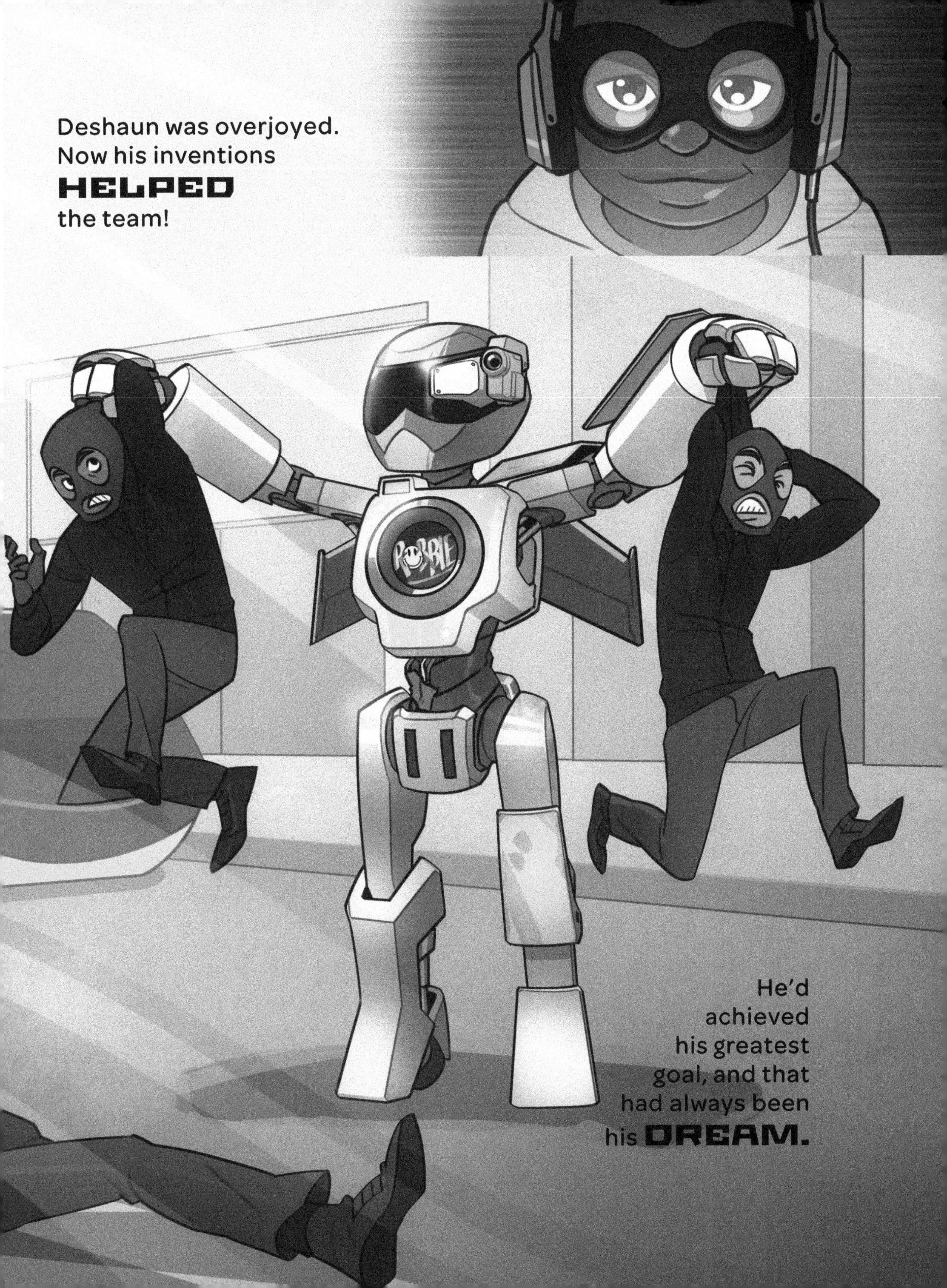
ROBBIE

He'd
achieved
his greatest
goal, and that
had always been
his **DREAM.**

Deshaun would not
forget the things that
Mom and Dad had said,

"All of us are gifted..."
The words echoed
in his head.

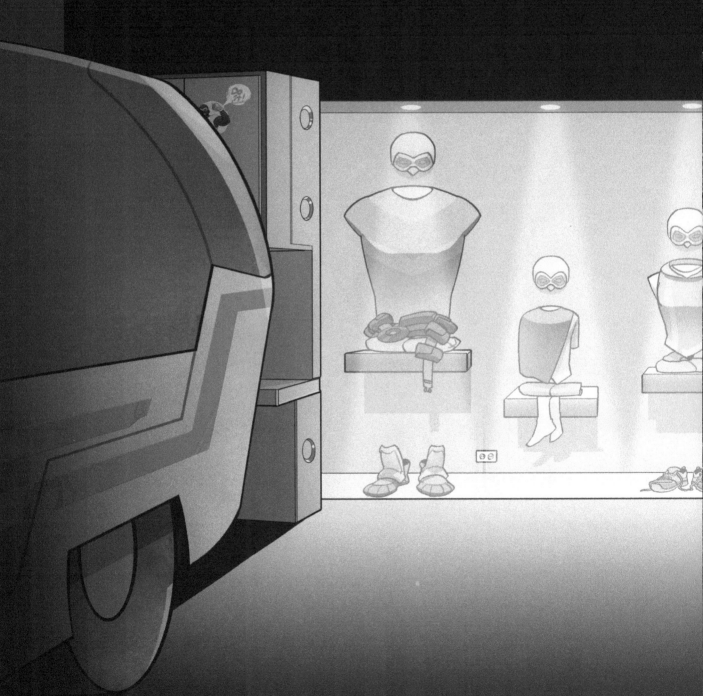

"Focus on the things that feel more natural to you.

The world one day will need a deed that only you can do."

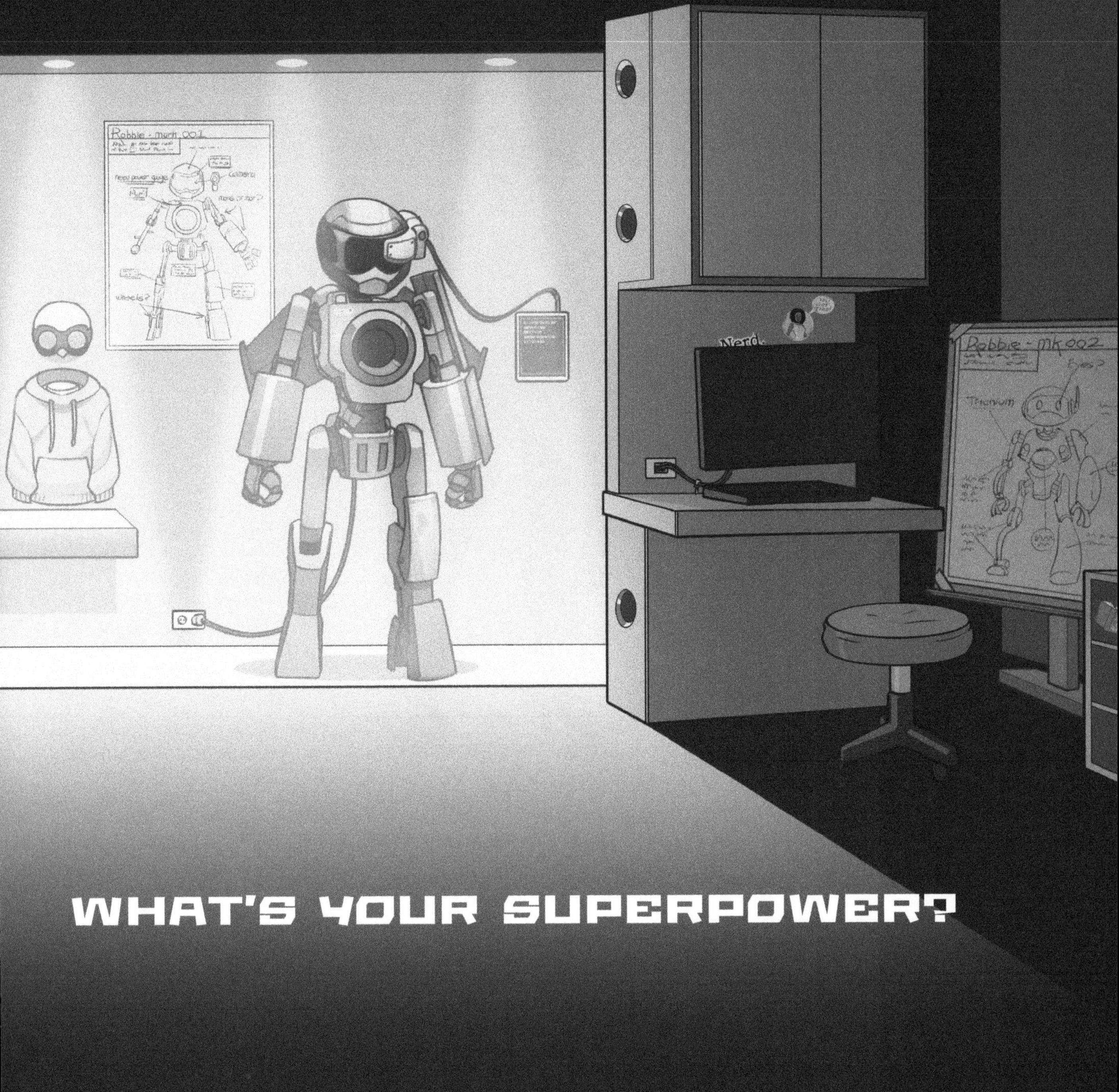

Robbie - mk 002
Nerd


# WHAT'S YOUR SUPERPOWER?

# FINDING YOUR UNIQUE SUPERPOWERS

**REMEMBER**
Mom and Dad's advice...

"The world one day will need a deed that only you can do. So, **FOCUS** on the things that feel more natural to you."

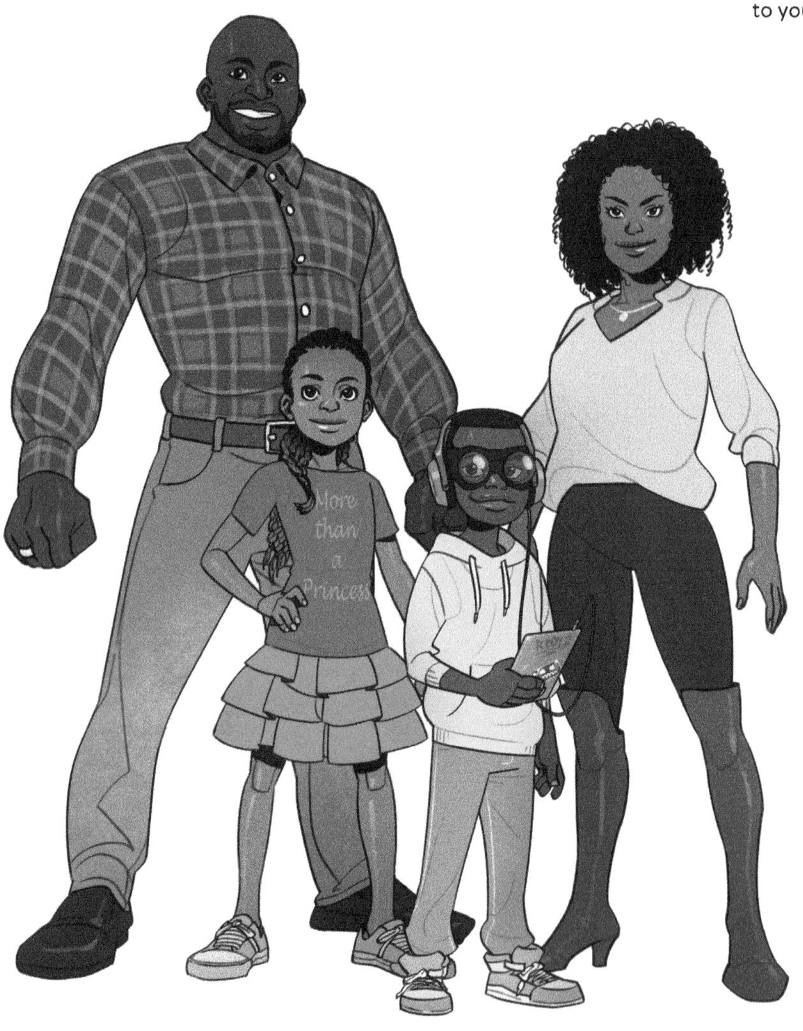
More than a Princess

**SHARE AND TALK**

about your superpowers with your family. Here is a list of possible superpowers!

1. Independent
2. Curious
3. Shares and takes turns
4. Is a good listener
5. Tells the truth and can apologize when needed
6. Likes talking to people
7. Uses lots of words and likes learning new words
8. Can sound out new words
9. Sees and understands patterns
10. Solves puzzles or word problems
11. Likes taking things apart and figuring out how they work
12. Can learn from mistakes and solve problems
13. Asks for help
14. Is creative
15. Likes drawing and sketching
16. Can dance, act, sing, or play a musical instrument
17. Can swim or play sports
18. Is gentle with animals and little kids
19. Tells funny jokes and stories
20. Likes playing video games

Everyone is born with a unique combination of
**SUPERPOWERS!**

Sometimes your superpower can be clear, like running really fast or reading really well. Other superpowers are harder to recognize - like being a team player or being caring and kind.

# THE ENGINEERING DESIGN PROCESS

**DESHAUN** followed the engineering design process to build Robbie. It helped him think critically, seek a solution and problem-solve.

You can use these steps to solve your hardest problems!

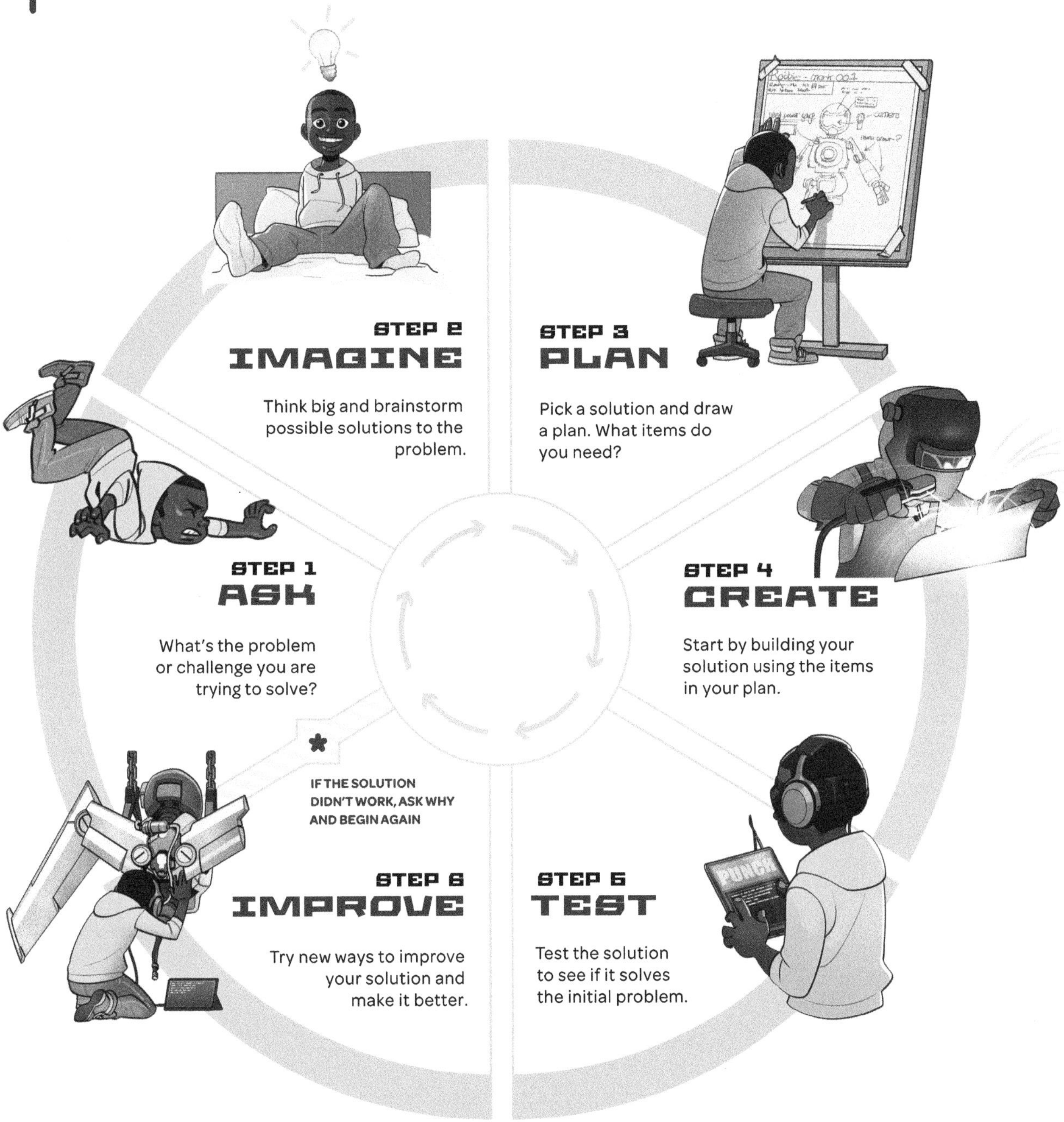
STEP 1
ASK
What's the problem or challenge you are trying to solve?
STEP 2
IMAGINE
Think big and brainstorm possible solutions to the problem.
STEP 3
PLAN
Pick a solution and draw a plan. What items do you need?
STEP 4
CREATE
Start by building your solution using the items in your plan.
STEP 5
TEST
Test the solution to see if it solves the initial problem.
STEP 6
IMPROVE
Try new ways to improve your solution and make it better.
*
IF THE SOLUTION DIDN'T WORK, ASK WHY AND BEGIN AGAIN
PUNCH

# ABOUT THE
# AUTHORS

## ❙ DELANDA COLEMAN

Delanda Coleman has spent over a decade as a leader in Product Marketing for some of the world's largest and most innovative software companies, including Microsoft and Brightcove. Having seen the fast-paced and evolving nature of technology, she was surprised by the lack of urgency or innovation in recruiting and developing women of color in the software industry. Inspired by the birth of her daughter, she and her husband, Terrence, decided to create Sydney and Coleman LLC to expose young black girls and boys to concepts and careers in STEAM (science, technology, engineering, art, and math).

A native and resident of Boston, MA, Delanda holds an MBA from New York University and a Bachelor's from Northeastern University. She is an avid reader and world traveler.

You can follow her on Instagram and Twitter @MsDelanda or learn more about her at DelandaColeman.com

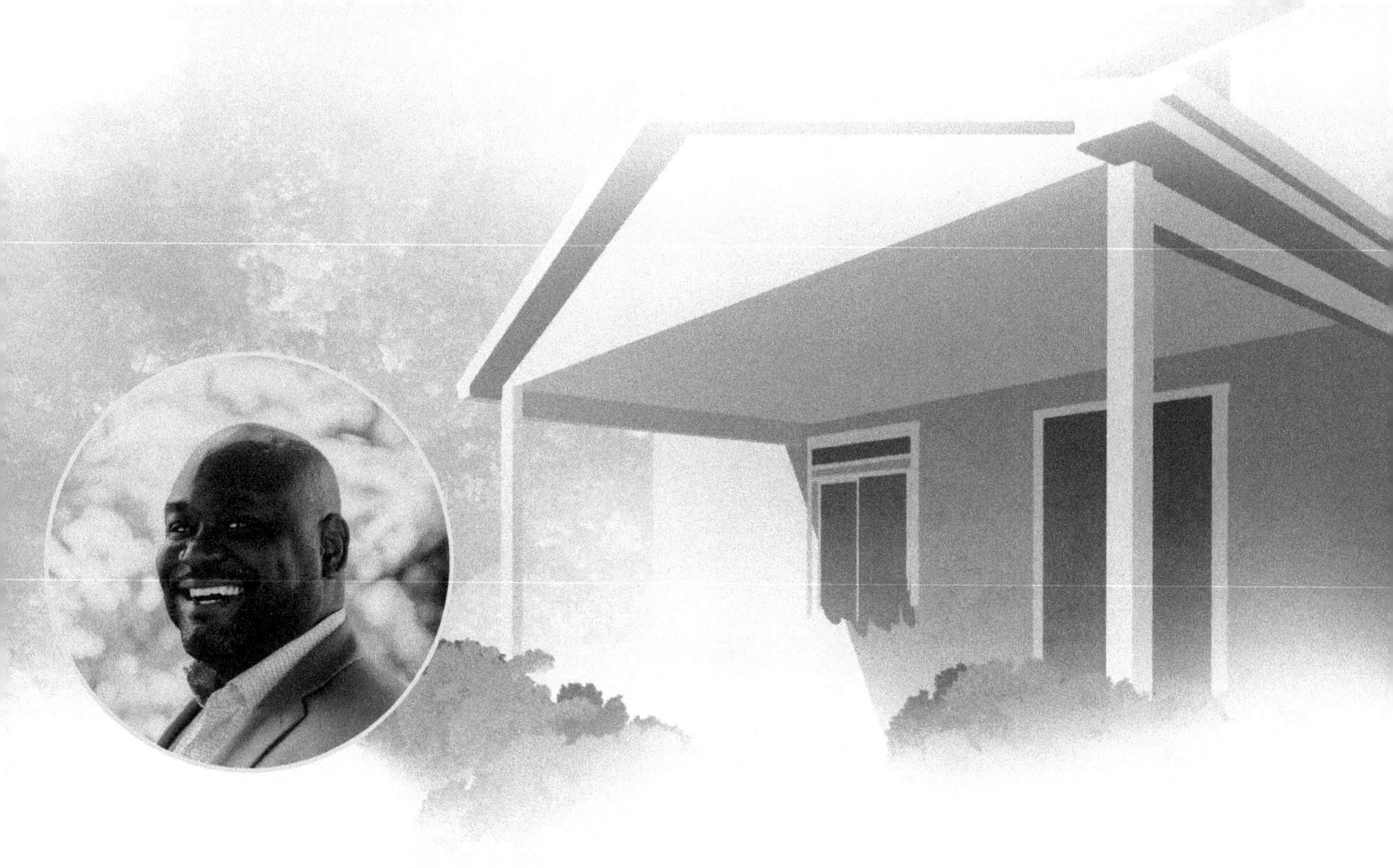

## TERRENCE COLEMAN

Terrence Coleman is a legal professional in the healthcare industry with a JD from Seattle University School of Law and a Bachelor's degree from Rutgers University. Much like his wife, Delanda, Terrence believes that there is a need to inspire children of color to pursue higher-level education. Sydney and Coleman Publishing focuses on promoting and advancing this need.

Terrence was raised in Willingboro, New Jersey, and enjoys reading, writing, and physical fitness.

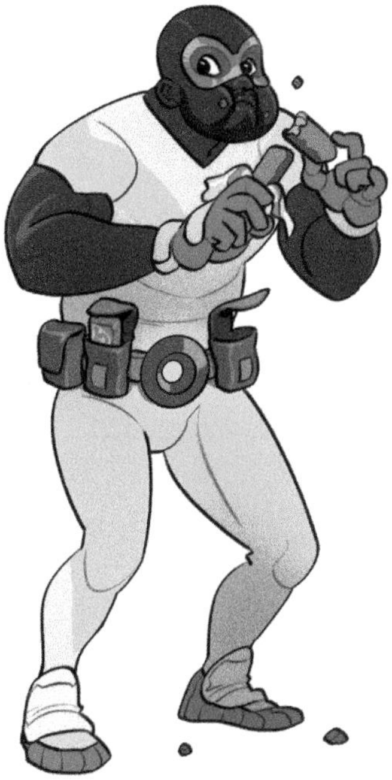

CPSIA information can be obtained
at www.ICGtesting.com
Printed in the USA
LVHW071249191222
735521LV00002B/121

9 781734 415858